PRAYING WITH THE SAINTS

Miraculous Prayers and Novenas for All Situations

UDEH ONYEKACHUKWU PATRICK

PRAYING WITH THE SAINTS

Copyright © 2011 Udeh Onyekachukwu Patrick

All rights reserved.

ISBN-13: 978-1466311794

DEDICATION

To Blessed Pope John Paul II, our friend in life and eternity.

PRAYING WITH THE SAINTS

PRAYING WITH THE SAINTS

CONTENTS

Acknowledgments — i

Introduction — 1

Litany of the Saints — 3

Part One: — 7

Erasmus, Benedict of Nursia, Anthony of Padua, Peter the Apostle, Alphonsus de Liguori, James the Great, Patrick, Anne, Gemma Galgani, Lucy of Syracuse

Part Two: — 32

Raphael the Archangel, Therese of Lisieux, Thomas the Apostle, Bernadette of Lourdes, Camillus of Lellis, Agatha of Sicily, Catherine of Siena, Peregrine Laziosi, Germaine Cousin, John of God

Part Three: — 49

Stanislaus Kostka, Pio, Michael the Archangel, Philomena, Teresa of Avila, Roch, Benedict Joseph Labre, Blaise, Vincent de Paul, Francis de Sales

Part Four: — 64

Andrew, Ignatius of Antioch, Anthony the Abbot, Christopher, Aloysius Gonzaga, Genesius of Rome, John Chrysostom, Vitus, Thomas Aquinas, Joseph

Part Five: — 86

Valentine of Rome, Martha of Bethany, Cecilia, Jude Thaddeus, Gerard, Rita of Cascia, Joan of Arc, Genevieve, Claire, Maria Goretti

PRAYING WITH THE SAINTS

ACKNOWLEDGMENTS

I am highly indebted to my family members for their patience and support while I worked on this collection; without them, this book would have remained a dream. My sincere gratitude also goes to Mary Imoko; she's indeed been a friend.

PRAYING WITH THE SAINTS

INTRODUCTION

God Works Wonders through His Saints

It is not uncommon to hear non-Catholic Christians voice their criticism of Catholic devotions to the saints. In fact, it is more common and driven with more commitment, than the public call to repentance.

We are often barraged by Bible quotes from Protestants who argue that it is wrong to pray through the saints since St. Paul called Christ our only Mediator with God the Father. They opine that prayers should be directed to God only through Jesus Christ, and that doing otherwise takes away the devotion due to God. But that isn't true.

The Acts of the Apostles show us many examples of God's intervention through the intercession of his saints, even when they were still on earth. The Apostles and deacons were given a share in God's own power, and performed great miracles. Acts 5: 15-16 tells us that people "even used to bring sick folk into the streets, and lay them down there on beds and pallets, in the hope that even the shadow of Peter, as he passed by might fall upon one of them here and there, and so they would be healed of their infirmities. From neighbouring cities, too, the common people flocked to Jerusalem, bringing with them the sick and those who were troubled by unclean spirits; and all of them were cured."

The saints, however, did not allow themselves to be worshiped; they made it clear that their power came from God (Acts 14: 10-14). Even at that, they did not rebuff those who came to them asking for miracles. And, in accordance with His promise, God granted many favours through their intercessions.

When holy men and women die and proceed into eternal glory, their power of intercession increases as they become perfect and more pleasing to God. In Heaven, the saints partake in the priestly role of Christ, mediating between humankind and God, praying for people and asking for forgiveness on their behalf (Rev. 20: 6).

So we can turn to the saints in Heaven, those great friends of God, asking them to pray for us. Wouldn't it be amazing if you could have an angel like St. Michael or St. Gabriel praying to God with you? And what about someone who has lived his or her life so devoutly like St. Pio of Petrelcina or St. Anthony of Padua, praying with you? The saints pray to God. We just ask them to pray for us.

When we honour the saints, we give glory to God, who sanctified them and worked (nay, works) wonders in them. These holy souls continue to intercede for devotees, obtaining countless favours for them every day.

Depending mostly on incidents during their lives, saints are often ascribed the special patronage of particular causes and subjects. Thus, there are patron saints for countries, professions, diseases and infirmities, states of life, and other situations.

There is St. Anthony for lost things, St. Jude for hopeless cases, St. Theresa for those suffering from Tuberculosis, St. Monica for troubled mothers, and so on.

This treasury of prayers and novenas to saints provides a handy resource for Catholics who seek the intercession of saints and the intervention of God in their various situations. *Praying With The Saints* aims to help Christians draw closer to God through His saints.

Litany of the Saints

Lord, have mercy on us. *Lord, have mercy on us.*
Christ, have mercy on us. *Christ, have mercy on us.*
Lord, have mercy on us. *Lord, have mercy on us.*
Christ, hear us. *Christ, graciously hear us.*

God, the Father of heaven, *have mercy on us.*
God the Son, Redeemer of the world, *have mercy on us.*
God the Holy Ghost, *have mercy on us.*
Holy Trinity, one God, *have mercy on us.*

Holy Mary, *pray for us.*
Holy Mother of God,
Holy Virgin of virgins,
Saint Michael,
Saint Gabriel,
Saint Raphael,
All ye holy angels and archangels,
All ye holy orders of blessed spirits,
Saint John the Baptist,
Saint Joseph,
All ye holy patriarchs and prophets,
Saint Peter,
Saint Paul,
Saint Andrew,
Saint James,
Saint John,
Saint Thomas,
Saint James,
Saint Philip,
Saint Bartholomew,
Saint Matthew,
Saint Simon,
Saint Thaddeus,
Saint Matthias,
Saint Barnabas,
Saint Luke,
Saint Mark,
All ye holy apostles and evangelists,
All ye holy disciples of the Lord,

All ye holy innocents,
Saint Stephen,
Saint Lawrence,
Saint Vincent,
Saints Fabian and Sebastian,
Saints John and Paul,
Saints Cosmos and Damian,
Saints Gervase and Protase,
All ye holy martyrs,
Saint Sylvester,
Saint Gregory,
Saint Ambrose,
Saint Augustine,
Saint Jerome,
Saint Martin,
Saint Nicholas,
All ye holy bishops and confessors,
All ye holy doctors,
Saint Anthony,
Saint Benedict,
Saint Bernard,
Saint Dominic,
Saint Francis,
All ye holy priests and levites,
All ye holy monks and hermits,
Saint Mary Magdalene,
Saint Agatha,
Saint Lucy,
Saint Agnes,
Saint Cecilia,
Saint Catherine,
Saint Anastasia,
Saint Clare,
All ye holy virgins and widows, *pray for us.*
All ye holy men and women, saints of God, *make intercession for us.*

Be merciful, *spare us, O Lord.*
Be merciful, *graciously hear us, O Lord.*

From all evil, *O Lord deliver us.*
From all sin,
From Thy wrath,
From sudden and unprovided death,

From the snares of the devil,
From anger, and hatred, and all ill-will,
From the spirit of fornication,
From the scourge of earthquake,
From plague, famine, and war,
From lightning and tempest,
From everlasting death,
Through the mystery of Thy holy Incarnation,
Through Thy coming,
Through Thy birth,
Through Thy baptism and holy fasting,
Through the Institution of the Most Blessed Sacrament,
Through Thy cross and passion,
Through Thy death and burial,
Through Thy holy resurrection,
Through Thine admirable Ascension,
Through the coming of the Holy Ghost the Paraclete,
In the day of judgment, *O Lord deliver us.*

We sinners, *we beseech Thee, hear us.*
That Thou wouldst spare us,
That Thou wouldst pardon us,
That Thou wouldst bring us to true penance,
That Thou wouldst vouchsafe to govern and preserve Thy holy Church,
That Thou wouldst vouchsafe to preserve our Apostolic Prelate and all orders of the Church in holy religion,
That Thou wouldst vouchsafe to humble the enemies of holy Church,
That Thou wouldst vouchsafe to give peace and true concord to Christian kings and princes,
That Thou wouldst vouchsafe to bring back to the unity of the Church all those who have strayed away, and lead to the light of the Gospel all unbelievers,
That Thou wouldst vouchsafe to confirm and preserve us in Thy holy service,
That Thou wouldst lift up our minds to heavenly desires,
That Thou wouldst render eternal blessings to all our benefactors,
That Thou wouldst deliver our souls, and the souls of our brethren, relatives, and benefactors from eternal damnation,
That Thou wouldst vouchsafe to give and preserve the fruits of the earth,
That Thou wouldst vouchsafe to grant eternal rest to all the faithful departed,
That Thou wouldst vouchsafe graciously to hear us,
Son of God, *we beseech Thee, hear us.*

Lamb of God, who takest away the sins of the world, *spare us, O Lord.*

Lamb of God, who takest away the sins of the world, *graciously hear us, O Lord.*
Lamb of God, who takest away the sins of the world, *have mercy on us.*

Let us pray.
Almighty, everlasting God, who hast dominion over both the living and the dead and art merciful to all who, as Thou foreknowest, will be Thine by faith and works; we humbly beseech Thee that they for whom we intend to pour forth our prayers, whether this present world still doth detain them in the flesh or the world to come hath already received them stripped of their mortal bodies, may, by the grace of Thy fatherly love and through the intercession of all the saints, obtain the remission of all their sins. Through our Lord Jesus Christ, Thy Son, who with Thee in the unity of the Holy Spirit liveth and reigneth God, world without end. Amen.

PART ONE

1
Saint Erasmus

Patronage: against abdominal pains, against appendicitis, against birth pains, against childhood intestinal disease, against colic, against danger at sea, against intestinal disorders, against seasickness, against stomach diseases, against storms, ammunition workers, boatmen, childbirth, explosives workers, mariners, navigators, ordnance workers, sailors, watermen and women in labour.

PRAYERS

Novena in Honour of Saint Erasmus

Preparatory Prayer
Almighty and eternal God! With lively faith and reverently worshiping Thy divine Majesty, I prostrate myself before Thee and invoke with filial trust Thy supreme bounty and mercy. Illumine the darkness of my intellect with a ray of Thy heavenly light and inflame my heart with the fire of Thy divine love, that I may contemplate the great virtues and merits of the saint in whose honor I make this novena, and following his example imitate, like him, the life of Thy divine Son.
Moreover, I beseech Thee to grant graciously, through the merits and intercession of this powerful Helper, the petition which through him I humbly place before Thee, devoutly saving, "Thy will be done on earth as it is in heaven."
Vouchsafe graciously to hear it, if it redounds to Thy greater glory and to the salvation of my soul. Amen.

Prayer in Honour of Saint Erasmus
O God, grant us through the intercession of Thy dauntless bishop and martyr Erasmus, who so valiantly confessed the faith, that we may learn the doctrine of this faith, practice its precepts, and thereby be made worthy to attain its promises.
We ask this through Christ our Lord. Amen.

Invocation of Saint Erasmus
Holy martyr Erasmus, who didst willingly and bravely bear the trials and sufferings of life, and by thy charity didst console many fellow-sufferers; I implore thee to remember me in my needs and to intercede for me with God. Staunch confessor of the Faith, victorious vanquisher of all tortures, pray Jesus for me and ask Him to grant me the grace to live and die in the Faith through which thou didst obtain the crown of glory. Amen.

Prayer
My LORD and my God! I offer up to Thee my petition in union with the bitter passion and death of Jesus Christ, Thy Son, together with the merits of His immaculate and blessed Mother, Mary ever virgin, and of all the saints, particularly with those of the holy Helper in whose honor I make this novena. Look down upon me, merciful Lord! Grant me Thy grace and Thy love, and graciously hear my prayer. Amen.

2
Saint Benedict of Nursia

Patronage: against erysipelas, against fever, against gall stones, against inflammatory diseases, against kidney disease, against nettle rash, against poison, against temptations, against witchcraft, agricultural workers, cavers, civil engineers, coppersmiths, dying people, farm workers, farmers, Italian architects, monks, people in religious orders, school children, servants who have broken their master's belongings, speliologists, spelunkers and students.

PRAYERS

Prayer to Saint Benedict
Admirable Saint and Doctor of Humility, you practiced what you taught, assiduously praying for God's glory and lovingly fulfilling all work for God and the benefit of all human beings. You know the many physical dangers that surround us today, often caused or occasioned by human inventions.

Guard us against poisoning of the body as well as of mind and soul, and thus be truly a "Blessed" one for us. Amen.

Prayer to Saint Benedict
Glorious Saint Benedict, sublime model of virtue, pure vessel of God's grace! Behold me humbly kneeling at your feet. I implore you in your loving kindness to pray for me before the throne of God. To you I have recourse in the dangers that daily surround me. Shield me against my selfishness and my indifference to God and to my neighbor. Inspire me to imitate you in all things. May your blessing be with me always, so that I may see and serve Christ in others and work for His kingdom.
Graciously obtain for me from God those favors and graces which I need so much in the trials, miseries and afflictions of life. Your heart was always full of love, compassion and mercy toward those who were afflicted or troubled in any way. You never dismissed without consolation and assistance anyone who had recourse to you. I therefore invoke your powerful intercession, confident in the hope that you will hear my prayers and obtain for me the special grace and favor I earnestly implore. *{ mention your petition}*
Help me, great Saint Benedict, to live and die as a faithful child of God, to run in the sweetness of His loving will, and to attain the eternal happiness of heaven. Amen.

Prayer for the Gifts to Seek God and Live in Him
Father, in your goodness, grant me the intellect to understand you, the perception to discern you, and the reason to appreciate you. In your kindness endow me with the diligence to look for you, the wisdom to discover you, and the spirit to apprehend you. In your graciousness bestow on me a heart to contemplate you, ears to hear you, eyes to see you, and a tongue to speak of you. In your mercy confer on me a conversation pleasing to you, the patience to wait for you, and the perseverance to long for you. Grant me a perfect end - your holy presence. Amen.

By Saint Benedict of Nursia, Monk and Founder of Benedictines

3
Saint Anthony of Padua

Patronage: against barrenness, against shipwreck, against starvation, against starving, against sterility, American Indians, amputees, animals, asses, boatmen, domestic animals, elderly people, expectant mothers, faith in the Blessed Sacrament, fishermen, harvests, horses, lost articles, lower animals, mail, mariners, oppressed people, paupers, poor people, pregnant women, sailors, seekers of lost articles, starving people, swineherds, travel hostesses, travelers, watermen, Brazil and Portugal

PRAYERS

Prayer to Saint Anthony the Wonder-Worker
Saint Anthony, perfect imitator of Jesus, who received from God the special power of restoring lost things, grant that I may find { *mention your petition*} which has been lost. As least restore to me peace and tranquility of mind, the loss of which has afflicted me even more than my material loss. To this favor I ask another of you: that I may always remain in possession of the true good that is God. Let me rather lose all things than lose God, my supreme good. Let me never suffer the loss of my greatest treasure, eternal life with God. Amen.

Prayer to Saint Anthony of Padua
Glorious Saint Anthony, my friend and special protector, I come to you with full confidence in my present necessity. In your overflowing generosity you hear all those who turn to you. Your influence before the throne of God is so effective that the Lord readily grants great favors at your request.
Please listen to my humble petition in spite of my unworthiness and sinfulness. Consider only your great and constant love for Jesus and Mary, and my desire for their glory and mercy. I beg you to obtain for me the grace I so greatly need, if it be God's will and for the good of my soul. I place this earnest petition in the care of the little mission children so that they may present it to you along their innocent prayers. Bless me, powerful Saint Anthony, in the name of the Father, and of the Son, and of the Holy Spirit. Amen.

Prayer to Saint Anthony of Padua
Glorious Saint Anthony, I salute you as a good servant of Christ, and a special friend of God. You once were favored to hold the Christ Child in your arms as you cherished His world in your heart. Today I place all my cares, temptations and anxieties in your hands. I resolve ever to honor you by imitating your example. Powerful patron, model of purity and victor over

fleshly impulses, please win for me, and for all devoted to you, perfect purity of body, mind and heart. I promise by my example and counsel to help others to the knowledge, love and service of God. Amen.

Prayer to Saint Anthony of Padua
Saint Anthony of Padua, you endured much discouragement in your life before finding your calling. Help us to find patience in our own lives, and to trust God to lead us where we need to go. You preached by example; help us show others through example the truth of our faith. Amen.

Prayer to Saint Anthony of Padua
Good Saint Anthony, in God's providence you have secured for His people many marvelous favors. You have been especially celebrated, good Saint Anthony, for your goodness to the poor and the hungry, for finding employment for those seeking it, for your special care of those who travel, and for keeping safe from harm all who must be away from home. You are widely known also, good Saint Anthony, for securing peace in the family, for your delicate mercy in finding lost things, for safe delivery of messages, and for your concern for women in childbirth. In honoring you, Saint Anthony, for the many graces our Lord grants through your favor, we trustfully and confidently ask your aid in our present need. Pray for us, good Saint Anthony, that we may be made worthy of the promises of Christ.

May it be a source of joy, O God, to your Church that we honor the memory of your Confessor and Doctor, Saint Anthony. May his spiritual help always make us strong, and by his assistance may we enjoy an eternal reward. This we ask through Jesus Christ, your Son, our Lord. Amen.

Prayer to Saint Anthony of Padua
Holy Saint Anthony, gentle and powerful in your help, your love for God and charity for His creatures, made you worthy, when on earth, to possess miraculous powers. Miracles waited on your word, which you were always ready to request for those in trouble or anxiety. Encouraged by this thought, I implore you to obtain for me [request]. The answer to my prayer may require a miracle. Even so, you are the Saint of miracles. Gentle and loving Saint Anthony, whose heart is ever full of human sympathy; take my petition to the Infant Savior for whom you have such a great love, and the gratitude of my heart will ever be yours. Amen.

Prayer to Saint Anthony of Padua
"Blessed be God in His Angels and in His Saints"
O Holy Saint Anthony, gentlest of Saints, your love for God and Charity for His creatures, made you worthy, when on earth, to possess miraculous

powers. Encouraged by this thought, I implore you to obtain for me [request]. O gentle and loving Saint Anthony, whose heart was ever full of human sympathy, whisper my petition into the ears of the sweet Infant Jesus, who loved to be folded in your arms; and the gratitude of my heart will ever be yours. Amen.

Prayer to Saint Anthony of Padua
O good and gentle Saint Anthony, your love of God and concern for His creatures made you worthy, while on earth, to possess miraculous powers. Come to my help in this moment of trouble and anxiety. Your ardent love of God you worthy to hold the Holy Infant in your arms. Whisper to Him my humble request, if it be for the greater glory of God, and the salvation of my soul. Amen.

Prayer to Saint Anthony, Consoler of the Afflicted
Dear Saint Anthony, comforting the sorrowful is a Christian duty and a work of mercy. By word, attitude, and deed I should try to brighten their days and make their burden easier to bear. Saint Anthony, *Consoler of the Afflicted*, may I remember when helping someone in sorrow that I am helping Christ Himself. Kindly mention my pressing needs to Him. *[Name your special intentions]*

Prayer to Saint Anthony of Padua, Disperser of Devils
Dear Saint Anthony, it is still as Saint Peter said: The devil prowls about, lion-like, looking for someone to devour. I confess that I don't always resist him; I sometimes toy with temptation. Saint Anthony, *Disperser of Devils*, remind me of my duty to avoid all occasions of sin. May I always pray in temptation that I may remain loyal to my Lord Jesus. Pray for my other intentions, please. *[Name them]*

Prayer to Saint Anthony of Padua, Example of Humility
Dear Saint Anthony, after all these years in the school of Christ, I still haven't learned the lesson of true humility. My feelings are easily ruffled. Quick to take offense, I am slow to forgive. Saint Anthony, *Example of Humility*, teach me the importance and necessity of this Christian virtue. In the presence of Jesus, who humbled Himself and whom the Father exalted, remember also these special intentions of mine. *[Name them]*

Prayer to Saint Anthony of Padua, Generator of Charity
Dear Saint Anthony, God wants us to see Christ, our brother, in everyone and love Him truly in word and in deed. God wills that we share with others the joy of His boundless love.

Saint Anthony, *Generator of Charity*, remember me in the Father's presence, that I may be generous in sharing the joy of His love. Remember also the special intentions I now entrust to you. *[Name them]*

Prayer to Saint Anthony of Padua, Guide of Pilgrims
Dear Saint Anthony, we are all pilgrims. We came from God and we are going to Him. He who created us will welcome us at journey's end. The Lord Jesus is preparing a place for all His brothers and sisters. Saint Anthony, *Guide of Pilgrims*, direct my steps in the straight path. Protect me until I am safely home in heaven. Help me in all my needs and difficulties. *[Name them]*

Prayer to Saint Anthony of Padua, Liberator of Prisoners
Dear Saint Anthony, I am imprisoned by walls of selfishness, prejudice, suspicion. I am enslaved by human respect and the fear of other people's opinions of me. Saint Anthony, *Liberator of Prisoners*, tear down my prison walls. Break the chains that hold me captive. Make me free with the freedom Christ has won for me. To your powerful intercession I also recommend these intentions. *[Name them]*

Prayer to Saint Anthony of Padua, Martyr of Desire
Dear Saint Anthony, you became a Franciscan with the hope of shedding your blood for Christ. In God's plan for you, your thirst for martyrdom was never to be satisfied. Saint Anthony, *Martyr of Desire*, pray that I may become less afraid to stand up and be counted as a follower of the Lord Jesus. Intercede also for my other intentions. *[Name them]*

Prayer to Saint Anthony of Padua, Model of Perfection
Dear Saint Anthony, you took the words of Jesus seriously, "Be perfect, even as your heavenly Father is perfect." The Church honors you as a Christian hero, a man wholly dedicated to God's glory and the good of the redeemed. Saint Anthony, *Model of Perfection*, ask Jesus to strengthen my good dispositions and to make me more like you, more like Him. Obtain for me the other favors I need. *[Name them]*

Prayer to Saint Anthony of Padua
Dear Saint Anthony, you are the patron of the poor and the helper of all who seek lost articles. Help me to find the object I have lost so that I will be able to make better use of the time I will gain for God's greater honor and glory. Grant your gracious aid to all people who seek what they have lost - especially those who seek to regain God's grace. Amen.

Prayer to Saint Anthony of Padua, Performer of Miracles
Dear Saint Anthony, your prayers obtained miracles during your lifetime. You still seem to move at ease in the realm of minor and major miracles. Saint Anthony, *Performer of Miracles*, please obtain for me the blessings God holds in reserve who serve Him. Pray that I may be worthy of the promises my Lord Jesus attaches to confident prayer. *[Mention your special intentions]*

Prayer to Saint Anthony of Padua, Restorer of Sight to the Blind
Dear Saint Anthony, you recall the Gospel episode about the blind man who, partly healed, could see men "looking like walking trees." After a second laying-on of Jesus' hands, he could see perfectly. Saint Anthony, *Restorer of Sight to the Blind*, please sharpen my spiritual vision. May I see people, not as trees or numbers, but as sons and daughters of the Most High. Help me in my pressing needs. *[Name your special intentions]*

Prayer to Saint Anthony of Padua, Restorer of Speech to the Mute
Dear Saint Anthony, how tongue-tied I can be when I should be praising God and defending the oppressed. My cowardice often strikes me dumb; I am afraid to open my mouth. Saint Anthony, *Restorer of Speech to the Mute*, release me from my fears. Teach me to praise God and to champion the rights of those unjustly treated. Please remember also all my intentions. *[Name them]*

Prayer to Saint Anthony of Padua, Reviver of the Dead
Dear Saint Anthony, I believe in the resurrection of the body. I have Christ's solemn pledge that whoever believes in Him, though he should die, shall live again. Saint Anthony, *Reviver of the Dead*, through your mighty prayers life was restored to the dead. Confirm my faith in the resurrection. Make me a confident Christian who expects a glorious Easter beyond the grave. Please take my need to God in prayer. *[Name your special intentions]*

Prayer to Saint Anthony the Wonder-Worker
Saint Anthony, you are glorious for your miracles and for the condescension of Jesus who came as a little child to lie in your arms. Obtain for me from His bounty the grace which I ardently desire. You were so compassionate toward sinners, do not regard my unworthiness. Let the glory of God be magnified by you in connection with the particular request that I earnestly present to you. *{ Mention your petition}*

As a pledge of my gratitude, I promise to live more faithfully in accordance with the teachings of the church, and to be devoted to the service of the poor whom you loved and still love so greatly. Bless this resolution of mine that I may be faithful to it until death.

Saint Anthony, consoler of all the afflicted, pray for me.
Saint Anthony, helper of all who invoke you, prays for me.
Saint Anthony, whom the Infant Jesus loved and honored so much, prays for me. Amen.

Prayer to Saint Anthony, Zealous for Justice
Dear Saint Anthony, you were prompt to fulfill all justice.
You gave God and His creation the service He required from you. You respected other people's rights and treated them with kindness and understanding. Saint Anthony, *Zealous for Justice*, teach me the beauty of this virtue. Make me prompt to fulfill all justice toward God and toward all creation. Help me also in my pressing needs. *[Name them]*

Litany to Saint Anthony of Padua
Lord, have mercy on us. *Lord, have mercy on us.*
Christ, have mercy on us. *Christ, have mercy on us.*
Lord, have mercy on us. *Lord, have mercy on us.*
Christ, hear us. *Christ, graciously hear us.*

God, the Father of Heaven, *have mercy on us.*
God, the Son, Redeemer of the world, *have mercy on us.*
God, the Holy Spirit, *have mercy on us.*
Holy Trinity, one God, *have mercy on us.*

Holy Mary, *pray for us.*
Saint Anthony of Padua, *pray for us.*
Saint Anthony, glory of the Friars Minor,
Saint Anthony, ark of the testament,
Saint Anthony, sanctuary of heavenly wisdom,
Saint Anthony, destroyer of worldly vanity,
Saint Anthony, conqueror of impurity,
Saint Anthony, example of humility,
Saint Anthony, lover of the Cross,
Saint Anthony, martyr of desire,
Saint Anthony, generator of charity,
Saint Anthony, zealous for justice,
Saint Anthony, terror of infidels,
Saint Anthony, model of perfection,
Saint Anthony, consoler of the afflicted,
Saint Anthony, restorer of lost things,
Saint Anthony, defender of innocence,
Saint Anthony, liberator of prisoners,

Saint Anthony, guide of pilgrims,
Saint Anthony, restorer of health.
Saint Anthony, performer of miracles,
Saint Anthony, restorer of speech to the mute,
Saint Anthony, restorer of hearing to the deaf,
Saint Anthony, restorer of sight to the blind,
Saint Anthony, disperser of devils,
Saint Anthony, reviver of the dead.
Saint Anthony, tamer of tyrants, *pray for us.*

From the snares of the devil, *Saint Anthony deliver us.*
From thunder, lightning and storms, *Saint Anthony deliver us.*
From all evil of body and soul, *Saint Anthony deliver us.*

Through your intercession, *Saint Anthony protect us.*
Throughout the course of life, *Saint Anthony protect us.*

Lamb of God, who takes away the sins of the world, *spare us, O Lord.*
Lamb of God, who takes away the sins of the world, *graciously hear us, O Lord.*
Lamb of God, who takes away the sins of the world, *have mercy on us.*

V. Saint Anthony, pray for us.
R. That we may be made worthy of the promises of Christ.

Let Us Pray: O my God, may the pious commemoration of Saint Anthony, your Confessor and Proctor, give joy to your Church, that she may ever be strengthened with your spiritual assistance and merit to attain everlasting joy. We pray through Christ our Lord. Amen.

4
Saint Peter the Apostle

Patronage: against feet problems, against fever, against foot problems, against frenzy, bakers, bridge builders, butchers, clock makers, cobblers, fishermen, harvesters, locksmiths, longevity, masons, net makers, papacy, popes, ship builders, shipwrights, shoemakers, stone masons, Universal Church and watch makers

PRAYERS

Prayer to Saint Peter
O Glorious Saint Peter, because of your vibrant and generous faith, sincere humility and flaming love our Lord honored you with singular privileges and especially leadership of the whole Church. Obtain for us the grace of a living faith, a sincere loyalty to the Church, acceptance of all her teaching, and obedience to all her precepts. Let us thus enjoy an undisturbed peace on earth and everlasting happiness in heaven. Amen.

5
Saint Alphonsus Maria de Liguori

Patronage: against arthritis, against scrupulosity, confessors, final perseverance, moralists, scrupulous people, theologians and vocations

PRAYERS

Prayer to Saint Alphonsus Liguori, patron of Moral Theologians
Precise and orthodox theologian, Master in theology of conduct, how greatly we need today theologians who are humble, prayerful, and eager to spread Christian conduct all around. You wrote much about the path to perfection and the means to follow the Teacher of all, who is the Way, the Truth, and the Life. Inspire our theologians to help the countless people who look to them for guidance in life's conduct.

Prayer of Saint Alphonsus Liguori to the Blessed Virgin
Most Holy and Immaculate Virgin! O my Mother! Thou who art the Mother of my Lord, the Queen of the world, the advocate, hope, and refuge of sinners! I, the most wretched among them, now come to thee. I worship thee, great Queen, and give thee thanks for the many favors thou hast bestowed on my in the past; most of all do I thank thee for having saved me from hell, which I had so often deserved. I love thee, Lady most worthy of all love, and, by the love which I bear thee, I promise ever in the future to serve thee, and to do what in me lies to win others to thy love. In thee I put all my trust, all my hope of salvation. Receive me as thy servant, and cover me with the mantle of thy protection, thou who art the Mother of mercy! And since thou hast so much power with God, deliver me from all temptations, or at least obtain for me the grace ever to overcome them. From thee I ask a true love of Jesus Christ, and the grace of a happy death. O my Mother! By thy love for God I beseech thee to be at all times my helper, but above all at the last moment of my life. Leave me not until thou seest me safe in heaven, there for endless ages to bless thee and sing thy praises. Such is my hope. Amen.

By Saint Alphonsus Maria de Liguori

Prayer of Alphonsus Maria de Liguori
O holy and heavenly Infant, Thou who art the destined Mother of my Redeemer and the great Mediatress of miserable sinners, pity me. Behold at thy feet another ungrateful sinner who has recourse to thee and asks thy compassion. It is true, that for my ingratitude to God and to thee, I deserve that God and thou should abandon me; but I have heard, and believe it to be so (knowing the greatness of thy mercy), that thou dost not refuse to help anyone who recommends himself to thee with confidence. O most exalted creature in the world! Since this is the case, and since there is no one but God above thee, so that compared with thee the greatest Saints of heaven are little; O Saint of Saints, O Mary, Abyss of charity, and full of grace, succour a miserable creature who by his own fault has lost the divine favour. I know that thou art so dear to God that He denies thee nothing. I know also that thy pleasure is to use thy greatness for the relief of miserable sinners. Ah, then, show how great is the favour that thou enjoyest with God, by obtaining me a divine light and flame so powerful that I may be changed from a sinner into a Saint; and detaching myself from every earthly affection, divine love may be enkindled in me. Do this, O Lady, for thou canst do it. Do it for the love of God, who has made thee so great, so powerful, and so compassionate. This is my hope. Amen.

By Saint Alphonsus Maria de Liguori

Prayer to Obtain Final Perseverance
Eternal Father, I humbly adore Thee, and thank Thee for having created me, and for having redeemed me through Jesus Christ. I thank Thee most sincerely for having made me a Christian, by giving me the true faith, and by adopting me as Thy son, in the sacrament of baptism. I thank Thee for having, after the numberless sins I had committed, waited for my repentance, and for having pardoned (as I humbly hope) all the offences which I have offered to Thee, and for which I am now sincerely sorry, because they have been displeasing to Thee, who art infinite goodness. I thank Thee for having preserved me from so many relapses, of which I would have been guilty if Thou hadst not protected me. But my enemies still continue, and will continue till death, to combat against me, and to endeavor to make me their slave. If Thou dost not constantly guard and succor me with thy aid, I, a miserable creature, shall return to sin, and shall certainly lose Thy grace. I beseech Thee, then, for the love of Jesus Christ, to grant me holy perseverance unto death. Jesus, Thy Son, has promised that Thou wilt grant whatsoever we ask in his name. Through the merits, then, of Jesus Christ, I beg, for myself and for all the just, the grace never again to be separated from Thy love, but to love Thee forever, in time and eternity. Mary, Mother of God, pray to Jesus for me.

By Saint Alphonsus Maria de Liguori

Prayer at the End of the Day
Jesus Christ my God, I adore you and I thank you for all the graces you have given me this day. I offer you my sleep and all the moments of this night, and I implore you to keep me safe from sin. To this end I place myself in your sacred side and under the mantle of our Lady, my Mother. Let your holy angels surround me and keep me in peace; and let your blessing be upon me. Amen.

By Saint Alphonsus Maria de Liguori

6
Saint James the Greater

Patronage: against arthritis, against rheumatism, apothecaries, arthritis sufferers, blacksmiths, equestrians, furriers, horsemen, knights, laborers, pharmacists, pilgrims, rheumatoid sufferers, riders, soldiers, Spanish conquistadors, tanners and veterinarians

PRAYERS

Prayer to Saint James the Greater
O Glorious Saint James, because of your fervor and generosity Jesus chose you to witness his glory on the Mount and his agony in the Garden. Obtain for us strength and consolation in the unending struggles of this life. Help us to follow Christ constantly and generously, to be victors over all our difficulties, and to receive the crown of glory in heaven. Amen.

7
Saint Patrick

Patronage: against ophidiophobia, against snake bites, against snakes, engineers, excluded people, ophidiophobics, Ireland and Nigeria

PRAYERS

Prayer for the Faithful by Saint Patrick
May the Strength of God guide us.
May the Power of God preserve us.
May the Wisdom of God instruct us.
May the Hand of God protect us.
May the Way of God direct us.
May the Shield of God defend us.
May the Angels of God guard us

-Against the snares of the evil one.

May Christ be with us!
May Christ be before us!
May Christ be in us!
Christ be over us all!

May Thy Grace, Lord,
Always be ours,
This day, O Lord, and forevermore. Amen.

Prayer for God's Protection and Christ's Presence
As I arise today, may the strength of God pilot me, the power of God uphold me, and the wisdom of God guide me. May the eye of God look before me, the ear of God hear me, the word of God speak for me. May the hand of God protect me, the way of God lie before me, the shield of God defend me, the host of God save me. May Christ shield me today...Christ with me, Christ before me, Christ behind me, Christ in me, Christ beneath me, Christ above me, Christ on my right, Christ on my left, Christ when I lie down, Christ when I sit, Christ when I stand, Christ in the heart of everyone who thinks of me, Christ in the mouth of everyone who speaks of me, Christ in every eye that sees me, Christ in every ear that hears me. Amen.

By Saint Patrick of Ireland, Bishop and Missionary

The Breastplate of Saint Patrick (the Cry of the Deer)
I arise today through a mighty strength, the invocation of the Trinity, through belief in the Threeness, through confession of the Oneness of the Creator of creation.

I arise today through the strength of Christ with His Baptism, through the strength of His Crucifixion with His Burial through the strength of His Resurrection with His Ascension, through the strength of His descent for the Judgment of Doom.

I arise today through the strength of the love of Cherubim in obedience of Angels, in the service of the Archangels, in hope of resurrection to meet with reward, in prayers of Patriarchs, in predictions of Prophets, in preaching of Apostles, in faiths of Confessors, in innocence of Holy Virgins, in deeds of righteous men.

I arise today, through the strength of Heaven: light of Sun, brilliance of Moon, splendour of Fire, speed of Lightning, swiftness of Wind, depth of Sea, stability of Earth, firmness of Rock.

I arise today, through God's strength to pilot me: God's might to uphold me, God's wisdom to guide me, God's eye to look before me, God's ear to hear me, God's word to speak for me, God's hand to guard me, God's way to lie before me,
God's shield to protect me, God's host to secure me: against snares of devils, against temptations of vices, against inclinations of nature, against everyone who shall wish me ill, afar and anear, alone and in a crowd.

I summon today all these powers between me (and these evils): against every cruel and merciless power that may oppose my body and my soul, against incantations of false prophets, against black laws of heathenry, against false laws of heretics, against craft of idolatry, against spells of women and smiths and wizards, against every knowledge that endangers man's body and soul. Christ to protect me today against poison, against burning, against drowning, against wounding, so that there may come abundance of reward.

Christ with me, Christ before me, Christ behind me, Christ in me, Christ beneath me, Christ above me, Christ on my right, Christ on my left, Christ in breadth, Christ in length, Christ in height, Christ in the heart of every man who thinks of me, Christ in the mouth of every man who speaks of me, Christ in every eye that sees me, Christ in every ear that hears me.

I arise today through a mighty strength, the invocation of the Trinity, through belief in the Threeness, through confession of the Oneness of the Creator of creation. Salvation is of the Lord. Salvation is of the Lord. Salvation is of Christ. May Thy Salvation, O Lord, be ever with us.

8
Saint Anne

Patronage: against poverty, against sterility, broommakers, cabinetmakers, carpenters, childless people, equestrians, expectant mothers, grandmothers, grandparents, homemakers, horse men, horse women, housewives, lace makers, lace workers, lost articles, miners, mothers, oldclothes dealers, poor people, pregnancy, pregnant women, riders, seamstresses, stablemen, turners and women in labour.

PRAYERS

Prayer to Saint Anne
Glorious Saint Anne, we think of you as filled with compassion for those who invoke you and with love for those who suffer. Heavily laden with the weight of my troubles, I cast myself at your feet and humbly beg of you to take the present affair which I commend to you under you special protection. *{ mention your petition}*
Deign to commend it to your daughter, our Blessed Lady, and lay it before the throne of Jesus, so that He may bring it to a happy conclusion. Cease not to intercede for me until my request is granted. Above all, obtain for me the grace of one day beholding my God face to face. With you and Mary and all the saints, may I praise and bless Him for all eternity.
Amen.
Good Saint Anne, mother of her who is our life, our sweetness and our hope, pray for me.

Prayer to Saint Anne
Good Saint Anne, you were especially favored by God to be the mother of the most holy Virgin Mary, the Mother of our Savior. By your power with your most pure daughter and with her divine Son, kindly obtain for us the grace and the favor we now seek. Please secure for us also forgiveness of our past sins, the strength to perform faithfully our daily duties and the help we need to persevere in the love of Jesus and Mary. Amen.

Prayer to Saint Anne
Dear Saint, we know nothing about you except your name.
But you gave us the Mother of God who called herself handmaid of the Lord. In your home you raised the Queen of Heaven and are rightly the model of homemakers. In your womb came to dwell the new Eve uniquely conceived without sin. Intercede for us that we too may remain free from sin. Amen.

Prayer to Saint Anne
Glorious Saint Anne, filled with compassion for those who invoke thee, and with love for those who suffer, heavily laden with the weight of my troubles, I cast myself at thy feet and humbly beg of thee to take the present affair which I recommend to thee under thy special protection.
Vouchsafe to recommend it to thy Daughter, the Blessed Virgin Mary, and lay it before the throne of Jesus, so that He may bring it to a happy issue. Cease not to intercede for me until my request is granted. Above all, obtain for me the grace of one day beholding my God face to face, and with Thee and Mary and all the Saints, praising and blessing Him to all eternity. Amen.

Prayer to Saint Anne
Families that are truly Christian love the Family of Nazareth, but they also honor the parents of Mary, especially Saint Anne who bore and gave birth to her. How glorious to give birth to one who would be the Mother of God! May we, who have devotion to you, Saint Anne, obtain even more devotion to Mary and the greatest devotion to Christ, your grandson.
Amen.

9
Saint Gemma Galgani

Patronage: against temptations, against the death of parents, against tuberculosis, apothecaries, druggists, pharmacists and students

PRAYERS
Saint Gemma Galgani's Prayer
O my crucified God, behold me at Your feet; do not cast me out, now that I appear before You as a sinner. I have offended You exceedingly in the past, my Jesus, but it shall be so no longer.

Before You, O Lord, I place all my sins; I have now considered Your own sufferings and see how great is the worth of that Precious Blood that flows from Your veins.

O my God, at this hour close Your eyes to my want of merit, and since You have been pleased to die for my sins, grant me forgiveness for them all, that I may no longer feel the burden of my sins, for this burden, Dear Jesus, oppresses me beyond measure.

Assist me, my Jesus, for I desire to become good whatsoever it may cost; take away, destroy, utterly root out all that You find in me contrary to Your holy will. At the same time, I pray You, Lord Jesus, to enlighten me that I may be able to walk in Your holy light. Amen.

Prayer of St. Gemma Galgani to Obtain a Desired Grace
Behold me at Your most holy feet, O dear Jesus, to manifest to you my gratitude for the continual favors which You have bestowed upon me, and still wish to bestow upon me. As many times as I have invoked You, O Jesus, You have made me content; I have often had recourse to You and You have always consoled me. How shall I express myself to You, dear Jesus? I thank you! Yet one more grace I desire of you, O my God, if it would be pleasing to You (*here mention your request*).
If you were not omnipotent, I would not make this request.
O Jesus, have pity on me. May your most holy will be done in all things"

Another Prayer from Saint Gemma to Jesus
O my crucified God, behold me at Your feet; do not cast me out, now that I appear before You as a sinner. I have offended You exceedingly in the past, my Jesus, but it shall be so no longer. Before You, O Lord, I place all my sins; I have now considered Your own sufferings and see how great is the worth of that Precious Blood that flows from Your veins. O my God, at this hour close Your eyes to my want of merit, and since You have been pleased to die for my sins, grant me forgiveness for them all, that I may no longer feel the burden of my sins, for this burden, dear Jesus, oppresses me beyond measure. Assist me, my Jesus, for I desire to become good whatsoever it may cost; take away, destroy, utterly root out all that You find in me contrary to Your holy will. At the same time, I pray You, Lord Jesus, to enlighten me that I may be able to walk in Your holy light.
Amen.

Novena to Saint Gemma Galgani

Day 1
Preface: Oh most Divine Lord, we humbly prostrate ourselves before Thy Infinite Majesty, and we adore Thee and dedicate to Thy glory the devout

prayers which we now present to Thee, as an act of devotion to your servant, St Gemma Galgani, whose intercession we are now imploring.
Most compassionate virgin, St. Gemma, during thy short life on earth, you gave a most beautiful example of angelic innocence and seraphic love and was found worthy to bear in thy flesh the marks of our Lord's Passion. Have pity on us who are so much in need of God's Mercy, and obtain for us through thy merits and intercession, the special favor which we now fervently implore *(mention request)*

Our Father, Hail Mary, Glory be.
Pray for us, Saint Gemma, that we may be made worthy of the promises of Christ.

Let us pray. O God, Who fashioned thy servant Saint Gemma into a likeness of Thy Crucified Son, grant us through her intercession the favor that we humbly request, and through the Passion Death and Resurrection of Thy Son, may we be united with You for all eternity. We ask this through Jesus Christ our Lord. Amen.

Day 2
Preface: Oh most Divine Lord, we humbly prostrate ourselves before Thy Infinite Majesty, and we adore Thee and dedicate to Thy glory the devout prayers which we now present to Thee, as an act of devotion to your servant, St Gemma Galgani, whose intercession we are now imploring.
O worthy Spouse of the Lamb of God and faithful virgin St Gemma, you preserved the innocence and splendor of virginity, giving to the world a bright example of purity and the most exalted virtues, look down with pity from thy high place in heaven upon us who confide in thee, as we implore thee for the favor we so ardently desire *(mention request)*

Our Father, Hail Mary, Glory be.
Pray for us, Saint Gemma, that we may be made worthy of the promises of Christ.

Let us pray. O God, Who fashioned thy servant Saint Gemma into a likeness of Thy Crucified Son, grant us through her intercession the favor that we humbly request, and through the Passion Death and Resurrection of Thy Son, may we be united with You for all eternity. We ask this through Jesus Christ our Lord. Amen

Day 3
Preface: Oh most Divine Lord, we humbly prostrate ourselves before Thy Infinite Majesty, and we adore Thee and dedicate to Thy glory the devout

prayers which we now present to Thee, as an act of devotion to your servant, St Gemma Galgani, whose intercession we are now imploring.
O most loving virgin St. Gemma, with an intense love for Jesus you suffered immensely for the conversion of sinners as a victim for sin, and you loved others intensely out of love for God. Do not forget us then, who remain here on earth, and look down with kindness on those of us who implore thee in the confident hope of receiving this favor through thy loving intercession *(mention request)*

Our Father, Hail Mary, Glory be.
Pray for us, Saint Gemma, that we may be made worthy of the promises of Christ.

Let us pray. O God, Who fashioned thy servant Saint Gemma into a likeness of Thy Crucified Son, grant us through her intercession the favor that we humbly request, and through the Passion Death and Resurrection of Thy Son, may we be united with You for all eternity. We ask this through Jesus Christ our Lord. Amen

Day 4
Preface: Oh most Divine Lord, we humbly prostrate ourselves before Thy Infinite Majesty, and we adore Thee and dedicate to Thy glory the devout prayers which we now present to Thee, as an act of devotion to your servant, St Gemma Galgani, whose intercession we are now imploring.
Blessed St Gemma, you who by the will of God suffered the loss of both of your parents at a young age, and whom also suffered countless pains in body and spirit, teach us how to sacrifice and to suffer out of love for God, that we too may expiate our sins here on earth, and thereby become more worthy of the infinite treasure of being united with God in heaven.

Our Father, Hail Mary, Glory be.
Pray for us, Saint Gemma, that we may be made worthy of the promises of Christ.

Let us pray. O God, Who fashioned thy servant Saint Gemma into a likeness of Thy Crucified Son, grant us through her intercession the favor that we humbly request *(mention request)*, and through the Passion Death and Resurrection of Thy Son, may we be united with You for all eternity. We ask this through Jesus Christ our Lord. Amen

Day 5
Preface: Oh most Divine Lord, we humbly prostrate ourselves before Thy Infinite Majesty, and we adore Thee and dedicate to Thy glory the devout

prayers which we now present to Thee, as an act of devotion to your servant, St Gemma Galgani, whose intercession we are now imploring.

Oh glorious St Gemma, for years you greatly desired to enter the consecrated religious life, but God desired otherwise, telling you after many years that it was not to be, and thereby causing you such great disappointment. Yet, you accepted this great sacrifice and resigned yourself to the will of God. Teach us then, dear St Gemma, to accept the sacrifices and sufferings that God permits in our lives, especially those that are very much against our own will and desires.

Our Father, Hail Mary, Glory be.
Pray for us, Saint Gemma, that we may be made worthy of the promises of Christ.

Let us pray. O God, Who fashioned thy servant Saint Gemma into a likeness of Thy Crucified Son, grant us through her intercession, the favor that we humbly request *(mention request)*, and through the Passion Death and Resurrection of Thy Son may we be united with You for all eternity. We ask this through Jesus Christ our Lord. Amen

Day 6
Preface: Oh most Divine Lord, we humbly prostrate ourselves before Thy Infinite Majesty, and we adore Thee and dedicate to Thy glory the devout prayers which we now present to Thee, as an act of devotion to your servant, St Gemma Galgani, whose intercession we are now imploring.

Beloved Gem of Christ St Gemma, whose heart was all on fire for the love of God, teach us to love God with all our hearts, minds and souls, and fervently place God above all things, so " that where our treasure is, there also will our heart be." (Matt 6:21)

Our Father, Hail Mary, Glory be.
Pray for us, Saint Gemma, that we may be made worthy of the promises of Christ.

Let us pray. O God, Who fashioned thy servant Saint Gemma into a likeness of Thy Crucified Son, grant us through her intercession, the favor that we humbly request *(mention request)*, and through the Passion Death and Resurrection of Thy Son may we be united with You for all eternity. We ask this through Jesus Christ our Lord. Amen

Day 7
Preface: Oh most Divine Lord, we humbly prostrate ourselves before Thy Infinite Majesty, and we adore Thee and dedicate to Thy glory the devout

prayers which we now present to Thee, as an act of devotion to your servant, St Gemma Galgani, whose intercession we are now imploring.
Oh holy saint of the Passion of Jesus, St Gemma, as a soul victim you were always pleading for the salvation of sinners.
Obtain for us, we beg you, not only the grace that we are asking, if it would be God's will *(mention request)* but most importantly obtain for us the conversion and salvation of our souls, so that someday we may be untied with Jesus, Mary and you for all eternity.

Our Father, Hail Mary, Glory be.
Pray for us, Saint Gemma, that we may be made worthy of the promises of Christ.

Let us pray. O God, Who fashioned thy servant Saint Gemma into a likeness of Thy Crucified Son, grant us through her intercession, the favor that we humbly request, and through the Passion Death and Resurrection of Thy Son may we be united with You for all eternity. We ask this through Jesus Christ our Lord. Amen

Day 8
Preface: Oh most Divine Lord, we humbly prostrate ourselves before Thy Infinite Majesty, and we adore Thee and dedicate to Thy glory the devout prayers which we now present to Thee, as an act of devotion to your servant, St Gemma Galgani, whose intercession we are now imploring.
Oh most fervent St Gemma, so many times you shed countless tears over your sins, and sought constantly to do penance and to make reparation for them. We who are so inclined to pamper ourselves, always seeking to gratify our senses and excuse ourselves from every penance, help us to recognize the infinite sufferings that Jesus endured for our sins, and all the pains we caused Him, and with the Passion of Jesus in mind, obtain for us a great sorrow and desire to never commit such sins again.

Our Father, Hail Mary, Glory be.
Pray for us, Saint Gemma, that we may be made worthy of the promises of Christ.

Let us pray. O God, Who fashioned thy servant Saint Gemma into a likeness of Thy Crucified Son, grant us through her intercession the favor that we humbly request *(mention request)*, and through the Passion Death and Resurrection of Thy Son, may we be united with You for all eternity. We ask this through Jesus Christ our Lord. Amen

Day 9
Preface: Oh most Divine Lord, we humbly prostrate ourselves before Thy Infinite Majesty, and we adore Thee and dedicate to Thy glory the devout prayers which we now present to Thee, as an act of devotion to your servant, Saint Gemma Galgani, whose intercession we are now imploring.
Oh most lovable St Gemma, we ask you to be our patroness and special friend today and always. Assist us in our daily spiritual and material needs and teach us to know, love and serve the Lord our God with all our hearts. Accompany us, along with our guardian Angel, in all our ways, and guide us lovingly to Heaven. Assist us at the time of our death along with Jesus, Mary and Joseph, and plead our cause before God, and trusting in His great mercy and the Passion of Jesus thy Spouse, obtain for us the salvation of our souls, and also the favor that we now humbly request *(mention request)*.

Our Father, Hail Mary, Glory be.
Pray for us, Saint Gemma, that we may be made worthy of the promises of Christ.

Let us pray. O God, Who fashioned thy servant Saint Gemma into a likeness of Thy Crucified Son, grant us through her intercession the favor that we humbly request, and through the Passion Death and Resurrection of Thy Son, may we be united with You for all eternity. We ask this through Jesus Christ our Lord. Amen.

10
Saint Lucy of Syracuse

Patronage: against blindness, against dysentery, against epidemics, against eye disease, against hemorraghes,
authors, blind people, cutlers, eye problems, glaziers, laborers, martyrs, peasants, saddlers, salesmen, sore eyes, sore throats, stained glass workers, throat infections and writers

PRAYERS

Prayer to Saint Lucy of Syracuse for Good Vision
Relying on Your goodness, O God, we humbly ask You, through the intercession of Saint Lucy, Virgin and Martyr, to give perfect vision to our eyes, that they may serve for Your greater honor and glory.
Saint Lucy, hear our prayers and obtain our petitions.
Amen.

Prayer to Saint Lucy of Syracuse
Dear Sicilian Virgin and Martyr, whom the Church recalls in Eucharistic Prayer I, you valiantly rejected great promises and resisted several threats in remaining faithful to your beloved Lord. For centuries Christians have invoked you particularly when suffering from eye trouble.
So now we implore your assistance on behalf of { *name of sufferer*}. We also ask you to teach us to imitate you and to avoid spiritual blindness of any kind.
Amen.

Prayer to Saint Lucy of Syracuse
Saint Lucy, your beautiful name signifies light. By the light of faith which God bestowed upon you, increase and preserve this light in my soul so that I may avoid evil, be zealous in the performance of good works, and abhor nothing so much as the blindness and the darkness of evil and of sin.
By your intercession with God, obtain for me perfect vision for my bodily eyes and the grace to use thme for God's greater honor and glory and the salvation of all men.
Saint Lucy, virgin and martyr, hear my prayers and obtain my petitions.
Amen.

Prayer to Saint Lucy of Syracuse
Saint Lucy, you did not hide your light under a basket, but let it shine for the whole world, for all the centuries to see.
We may not suffer torture in our lives the way you did, but we are still called to let the light of our Christianity illumine our daily lives. Please help us to have the courage to bring our Christianity into our work, our recreation, our relationships, and our conversation -- every corner of our day.
Amen.

PART TWO

11
Saint Raphael the Archangel

Patronage: against bodily ills, against eye disease, against eye problems, against insanity, against mental illness, against nightmares, against sickness, apothecaries, blind people, doctors, druggists, guardian angels, happy meetings, love, lovers, mentally ill people, nurses, pharmacists, physicians, shepherdesses, shepherds, sick people, travellers and young people

PRAYERS

Prayer to Saint Raphael
Dear Saint Raphael, your lovely name means "God heals." The Lord sent you to young Tobias to guide him throughout a long journey. Upon his return you taught him how to cure his father's blindness. How natural, therefore, for Christians to pray for your powerful help for safe travel and a happy return. This is what we ask for ourselves as well as for all who are far from home.

Prayer to Saint Raphael the Archangel
Glorious Archangel Saint Raphael, great prince of the heavenly court, you are illustrious for your gifts of wisdom and grace. You are a guide of those who journey by land or sea or air, consoler of the afflicted, and refuge of sinners. I beg you, assist me in all my needs and in all the sufferings of this life, as once you helped the young Tobias on his travels. Because you are the "medicine of God," I humbly pray you to heal the many infirmities of my soul and the ills that afflict my body. I especially ask of you the favor { *mention your petition*} and the great grace of purity of prepare me to be the temple of the Holy Spirit. Amen.
Saint Raphael of the glorious seven who stand before the throne of Him who lives and reigns, angel of health, the Lord has filled your hand with balm from heaven to soothe or cure our pains. Heal or cure the victim of disease, and guide our steps when doubtful of our ways.

Prayer for the Protection of Saint Raphael
O God who in Thy ineffable goodness hast rendered blessed Raphael the conductor of thy faithful in their journeys, we humbly implore Thee that we may be conducted by him in the way of salvation, and experience his help in the maladies of our souls. We ask this through Jesus Christ, Our Lord. Amen.

Prayer to Saint Raphael
O Raphael, lead us toward those we are waiting for, those who are waiting for us: Raphael, Angel of happy meeting, lead us by the hand toward those we are looking for. May all our movements be guided by your Light and transfigured with your joy.

Angel, guide of Tobias, lay the request we now address to you at the feet of Him on whole unveiled Face you are privileged to gaze. Lonely and tired, crush by the separations and sorrows of life, we feel the need of calling you and of pleading for the protection of your wings, so that we may not be as strangers in the province of joy, all ignorant of the concerns of our country. Remember the weak, you who are strong, you whose home lies beyond the region of thunder, in a land that is always peaceful, always serene and bright with the resplendent glory of God.

Litany of Saint Raphael
Lord, have mercy on us. *Lord, have mercy.*
Christ, have mercy on us. *Christ, have mercy.*
Lord, have mercy on us. *Lord, have mercy.*
Christ, hear us. *Christ, graciously hear us.*
God the Father of Heaven, *Have mercy on us.*
God the Son, Redeemer of the world, *Have mercy on us.*
God the Holy Spirit, *Have mercy on us.*
Holy Trinity, One God, *Have mercy on us.*

Holy Mary, Queen of Angels, *pray for us.*
Saint Raphael, *pray for us.*
Saint Raphael, filled with the mercy of God,
Saint Raphael, perfect adorer of the Divine Word,
Saint Raphael, terror of demons,
Saint Raphael, exterminator of vices,
Saint Raphael, health of the sick,
Saint Raphael, our refuge in all our trials,
Saint Raphael, guide of travelers,
Saint Raphael, consoler of prisoners,
Saint Raphael, joy of the sorrowful,
Saint Raphael, filled with zeal for the salvation of souls,
Saint Raphael, whose name means *God heals*,
Saint Raphael, lover of chastity,
Saint Raphael, scourge of demons,
Saint Raphael, in pestilence, famine and war,
Saint Raphael, angel of peace and prosperity,
Saint Raphael, endowed with the grace of healing,
Saint Raphael, sure guide in the paths of virtue and sanctification,

Saint Raphael, help of all those who implore your assistance,
Saint Raphael, who was the guide and consolation of Tobias on his journey,
Saint Raphael, whom the Scriptures praise: *Raphael, the holy angel of the Lord, was sent to cure,*
Saint Raphael, our advocate,

Lamb of God, Who takes away the sins of the world,
Spare us, O Lord.
Lamb of God, Who takes away the sins of the world,
Graciously hear us, O Lord.
Lamb of God, Who takes away the sins of the world,
Have mercy on us.
Christ, hear us.
Christ, graciously hear us.

Pray for us, Saint Raphael, to the Lord Our God,
That we may be made worthy of the promises of Christ

Let Us Pray: Lord, Jesus Christ, by the prayer of the Archangel Raphael, grant us the grace to avoid all sin and to persevere in every good work until we reach our heavenly destination, You Who lives and reigns world without end. Amen.

12
Saint Therese of Lisieux

Patronage: African missions, against bodily ills, against illness, against sickness, AIDS patients, air crews, aircraft pilots, Australia, aviators, black missions, florists, flower growers, loss of parents, missionaries, parish missions, restoration of religious freedom in Russia, sick people and tuberculosis

PRAYERS

Prayer to Saint Theresa of the Child Jesus
Dear Little Flower of Lisieux, how wonderful was the short life you led. Though cloistered, you went far and wide through fervent prayers and great sufferings. You obtained from God untold helps and graces for his evangelists. Help all missionaries in their work and teach all of us to spread Christianity in our own neighborhoods and family circles.
Amen.

Invocation to Saint Theresa
O Little Flower of Jesus, ever consoling troubled souls with heavenly graces, in your unfailing intercession I place my trust. From the Heart of Our Blessed Savior petition these blessing of which I stand in greatest need *(mention here)*. Shower upon me your promised roses of virtue and grace, dear Saint Therese, so that swiftly advancing in sanctity and in perfect love of neighbor, I may someday receive the crown of eternal life. Amen.

Novena to Saint Therese of the Child Jesus
O Little Therese of the Child Jesus, please pick for me a rose from the heavenly gardens and send it to me as a message of love.
O Little Flower of Jesus, ask God today to grant the favors I now place with confidence in your hands... *(mention specific request)* Saint Therese, help me to always believe as you did, in God's great love for me, so that I might imitate your "Little Way" each day.
Amen.

Novena to Saint Therese of the Little Flower
Saint Therese, the Little Flower, please pick me a rose from the heavenly garden and send it to me with a message of love.
Ask God to grant me the favor I thee implore and tell Him I will love Him each day more and more.
(The above prayer, plus 5 Our Father's, 5 Hail Mary's and 5 Glory Be's must be said on 5 successive days, before 11 a.m. On the 5th day, the 5th set of prayers having been completed, offer one more set - 5 Our Father's, 5 Hail Mary's and 5 Glory Be's.)

Novena to Saint Theresa the Little Flower

First Day
O Heavenly Father, Who in Thy ineffable goodness didst place in the soul of Saint Theresa of the Child Jesus the precious treasure of sanctifying grace, and didst grant her ever to keep it in the midst of earthly dangers, we pray Thee to grant to us for our part the happiness of never losing this inestimable

gift whereby we become Thy adopted children, the brothers and sisters of Thy Son Jesus, the temples of the Holy Spirit and the heirs of Heaven. Enable us, to this end, carefully to avoid mortal sin which would rob us of this grace more to be desired than all the wealth of the world, to fly the occasions of sin, and to resist temptation. We implore these graces through the intercession of the one who was ever Thy faithful child and whose memory we venerate.

Saint Theresa of the Child Jesus, who would have preferred to die rather than lose God's grace, vouchsafe to obtain for us all the help necessary to avoid the misfortune of committing mortal sin, incompatible with this divine grace. Obtain for us the favors we crave and implore through you powerful intercession. Amen.

Second Day
O Heavenly Father, Who to assure our advancement in the right path dost never cease to multiply the supernatural means of help which we need, and which Thou has divinely poured out upon Saint Theresa of the Child Jesus, we beg of Thee, through this Saint so dear to Thy Heart, all the graces of light and of fortitude necessary or helpful to fulfill Thy adorable will. Thy grace ever went before Saint Theresa and Thou didst uphold her at each moment, for Thou didst give to her both to will and to do, and without Thee none can even utter the name of Jesus whereby we may be saved.

Father, shed abroad in our minds and hearts those graces won by the merits of our Savior and which Saint Theresa asks for us.

Saint Theresa of the Child Jesus upon whom so many divine graces were showered, we pray you to intercede with our Heavenly Father, so that through the merits of our Savior and you merits, He may vouchsafe to give to our souls all the graces needful for the perfect fulfillment of our duty. Obtain for us the favors we crave and implore through your powerful intercession. Amen.

Third Day
O Heavenly Father, Who didst dispose the soul of Saint Theresa of the Child Jesus to ascend by such wonderful steps and didst make this lovable saint to rise from virtue to virtue, aiding her so admirably to practice humility, simplicity, patience, confidence, zeal and love, we beseech Thee to place in our hearts dispositions like to hers and to grant us to resemble her, that we may hence become conformable to Thy Son Jesus, our Model and the Divine Example of Thy adorable perfections. These virtues are so needful for us, for without them we cannot be happy here below; without them we cannot gain for Thee the glory that Thou dost look for from us.

Vouchsafe, O Father, to help us to make these virtues ours. May Thy numerous graces joined to our generous efforts, bring forth, as in Saint Theresa, true and lasting virtue.

Saint Theresa of the Child Jesus who to please God ever wonderfully grew in virtue each day of your life, obtain for us to resemble you and generously to practice those virtues of which you have left us such a beautiful example. Obtain for us the favors we crave and implore through your powerful intercession. Amen.

Fourth Day
O Heavenly Father, Who in Thy infinite wisdom dost permit the just to be tried upon earth, like gold in the furnace, hereafter to crown them gloriously in Heaven, we beseech Thee to grant us through the intercession of Saint Theresa of the Child Jesus, all the graces of fortitude and consolation which we urgently need in the difficulties we encounter here below. Thou dost order all things for the good of those who love Thee, nothing befalls without Thy permission, Thou knowest how to draw good out of evil. May these consoling truths be our support in the midst of our sorrows. Sweeten for us all that is bitter by the unction of Thy grace.

Permit not, O Father, that impatience shall possess our heart or murmurs rise to our lips. Make us understand the providential use of sorrow, as it was undertook by Saint Theresa who owned to finding happiness in the midst of suffering.

Saint Theresa of the Child Jesus who suffered much here below, and knew how to find joy in every bitterness, intercede for us with God that so He may help us to bear patiently all our crosses, and console our hearts saddened by the trials of earth's exile. Obtain for us the favors we crave and implore through your powerful intercession.
Amen.

Fifth Day
O Heavenly Father, Who so loved men that Thou didst give them Thy Only-begotten Son to be their Redeemer upon the Cross, and Food in the Divine Sacrament of the Altar, we beseech Thee to grant us, through the prayers of Saint Theresa of the Child Jesus so inflamed with love for this Adorable Sacrament and so eager to receive It, the grace for our part to draw near very often to the Holy Table.

Following the example of Saint Theresa of the Child Jesus, may we bring to it the best dispositions, a right intention, hearts filled with lively faith, sincere humility, deep confidence, ardent charity.

Father, make us truly understand that this Divine Bread is no less needful to our soul than material bread is to our body and that we cannot abstain from It without hurt to our soul.

Saint Theresa of the Child Jesus who so much loved the Divine Sacrament of the Altar and so greatly longed to unite yourself to It through Holy Communion, obtain for us from God a love like to yours for this Adorable Sacrament and a fervent longing often to receive It in our hearts.
Obtain for us the favors we crave and implore through your powerful intercession. Amen

Sixth Day
O Heavenly Father, Who bestowed upon the Blessed Virgin Mary the greatest and most precious graces and privileges, and called her to become the Mother of Thy Son Jesus also giving her to be our Mother, we beseech Thee through the intercession of Saint Theresa of the Child Jesus ever so faithful to honor this beloved Virgin, whose radiant countenance and gracious smile she one day beheld, to grant us too the inestimable favor of being the very loving children of this Holy Mother.
We need her maternal mediation, for this good Mother is the way that leads to Jesus, and she is the treasurer of all the graces that our Savior acquired for us by shedding of His Precious Blood.
We thank Thee, O Father, for having given us the Blessed Virgin to be our Mother, and our guide along our life's path, and we beseech Thee that, like Saint Theresa of the Child Jesus, we may be true imitators of her virtues: of her perfect humility, her immaculate purity, and her ardent love. We look to her for the greatest succor now and at the hour of our death.
Saint Theresa of the Child Jesus who ever manifested a great love for the One you named the Immaculate Virgin, and from whom you received so many benefits, we ask you to obtain for us the grace to imitate your tender devotion towards her and to help us to reproduce her beautiful and admirable virtues even as you yourself did. Obtain for us the favors we crave and implore through your powerful intercession. Amen.

Seventh Day
O Heavenly Father, Who has bestowed upon us so many benefits through the intercession of Saint Theresa of the Child Jesus, and willest that we should honor this lovable saint with a special devotion, we earnestly implore Thee of Thy fatherly loving-kindness the grace to be ever faithful in venerating her, invoking her and imitating her virtues.
It is good for us to pay honor to the Saints. Thou has placed these blessed Saints as powerful mediators between ourselves and Thee, that so Thou mayest bestow upon us more ready and more abundant aids. That which our prayer cannot obtain, theirs will obtain for us. Thou hast willed that the Saints should be our models. They were once what we are; we can with Thy grace become what they are, what they have done, we can do in our turn.

Father, give us a true and lasting devotion towards Saint Theresa of the Child Jesus, a devotion well-ordered and constant, a devotion that will sanctify us and lead us to Thee to Whom all the homage we pay to the Saints returns. Saint Theresa of the Child Jesus, placed by the Church upon our altars to be out protectress with God and model in Christian life, obtain for us, we ask of you, ever to have you in honor, to venerate you, to invoke you, to imitate you for the greater glory of God and the greater good of our souls. Obtain for us the favors we crave and implore through your powerful intercession. Amen.

Eighth Day

O Heavenly Father, Who hast created all the good things of earth for the use of man and dost measure them out to him with marvelous bounty, we beg Thee through the intercession of Saint Theresa of the Child Jesus to give us all those things of which we have need for the preservation of our life here below.

Teach us to use these things with the moderation befitting Christians, let us not attach our heart to them; may they serve not to keep us from Thee, the Only True Good to be desired and the Giver of all that is good in this world. Give us, as Thou gavest to Thy faithful handmaid Saint Theresa of the Child Jesus, to make a holy use of earthly things and to make them serve on for Thy Glory.

Father, Who dost feed the birds of the air and clothe the lilies of the valley, forsake not the souls of those who trust in Thee.

Saint Theresa of the Child Jesus who ever used the things of this world according to the order willed by God, you who made earthly gifts serve to merit those that are heavenly, we ask you to obtain for us all that is necessary for us during our life upon earth. Obtain for us the favors we crave and implore through your powerful intercession. Amen.

Ninth Day

O Heavenly Father, Who hast prepared for us a glorious reward after the labors of this life, and hast promised to crown with honor and glory those who are faithful to the end in Thy love, we beseech Thee to grant us through the intercession of Saint Theresa of the Child Jesus the grace to be faithful to Thy Commandments, to those of the Holy Church and to Thy holy inspirations until the hour of our death.

Father, grant that, after the example of Saint Theresa of the Child Jesus, we may not recoil from labors, that temptations may not keep us from Thee, that trials may not cause us to lose courage. May neither the world, nor the devil, nor our own inclinations separate us from Thee to Whom we desire to belong forever, as we promised Thee on the day of our Baptism and on the day of our First Communion.

Perseverance in grace is a grace, we beseech Thee to grant it to us, and in Thy merciful love not to refuse us the grace of graces, that of final perseverance which will unite us to
Thee for evermore and will give us to contemplate during all Eternity Thy adorable Face.
Father, uphold us in the midst of our combats until the day when we shall gain the victory, when Thou Thyself wilt triumph in us.
Saint Theresa of the Child Jesus who persevered throughout your life in exact fidelity to God's grace, you who saw your perseverance crowned own the glorious day of your death, obtain for us to be fully faithful to God's law and never to separate ourselves from His holy love. Obtain for us the favors we crave and implore through your powerful intercession. Amen.

13
Saint Thomas the Apostle

Patronage: against blindness, against doubt, architects, builders, construction workers, geometricians, India, masons, Pakistan, people in doubt, Sri Lanka, stone masons, stonecutters, surveyors and theologians

PRAYERS

Prayer to Saint Thomas the Apostle
O Glorious Saint Thomas, your grief for Jesus was such that it would not let you believe he had risen unless you actually saw him and touched his wounds. But your love for Jesus was equally great and it led you to give up your life for him. Pray for us that we may grieve for our sins which were the cause of Christ's sufferings. Help us to spend ourselves in his service and so earn the title of "blessed" which Jesus applied to those who would believe in him without seeing him. Amen.

Prayer to Saint Thomas the Apostle
Dear Saint Thomas, you were once slow in believing that Christ had gloriously risen; but later, because you had seen him, you exclaimed: "My Lord and my God!" According to an ancient story, you rendered most powerful assistance for constructing a church in a place where pagan priests opposed it. Please bless architects, builds and carpenters that through them the Lord may be honored. Amen.

14

Saint Bernadette of Lourdes

Patronage: against bodily ills, against illness, against poverty, against sickness, Lourdes, France, people ridiculed for their piety, poor people, shepherdesses, shepherds and sick people

PRAYERS

Prayer to Saint Bernadette of Lourdes
O God, protector and lover of the humble, You bestowed on Your servant, Bernadette, the favor of the vision of Our Lady, the Immaculate Virgin Mary, and of speech with her.
Grant that we may deserve to behold You in heaven. Amen.

Novena to Saint Bernadette
(Say for nine days, or as a perpetual novena)
Dear Saint Bernadette, Chosen by Almighty God as a channel of His Graces and Blessings, and through your humble obedience to the requests of Our Blessed Mother, Mary, you gained for us the Miraculous waters of Spiritual and physical healing.

We implore you to listen to our pleading prayers that we may be healed of our Spiritual and physical imperfections. Place our petitions in the Hands of our Holy Mother, Mary, so that She may place them at the feet of Her beloved Son, Our Lord and Saviour Jesus Christ, that He may look on us with mercy and compassion: *(make petition)* Help, O Dear Saint Bernadette to follow your example, so that irrespective of our own pain and suffering we may always be mindful of the needs of others, especially those whose sufferings are greater than ours.

As we await the Mercy of God, remind us to offer up our pain and suffering for the conversion of sinners, and in reparation for the sins and blasphemies of mankind.

Pray for Saint Bernadette, that like you, we may always be obedient to the will of Our Heavenly Father, and that through our prayers and humility we may bring consolation to the Most Sacred Heart of Jesus and the Immaculate Heart of Mary that have been so grievously wounded by our sins.

Holy Saint Bernadette of Lourdes, Pray for us.

(One Decade of the Rosary)
(The Memorare)

O Mary conceived without sin, pray for us who have recourse to Thee. *(Say three times)*

15

Saint Camillus of Lellis

Patronage: against bodily ills, against illness, against sickness, hospitals, hospital workers, nurses and sick people

PRAYERS

Prayer to Saint Camillus of Lellis
Most wonderful Saint, your compassion for the sick and the dying led you to found the Servants of the Sick. As the Patron of nurses and hospital workers, infuse in them your compassionate spirit. Make hospitals resemble the inn in

Christ's Parable to which the Good Samaritan brought the wounded man saying: "Take care of him and I will repay you for it." Amen.

16

Saint Agatha of Sicily

Patronage: against breast cancer, against breast disease, against earthquakes, against eruptions of Mount Etna, against fire, against natural disasters, against sterility, against volcanic eruptions, bell-founders, fire prevention, jewelers, martyrs, nurses, rape victims, single laywomen, torture victims and wet-nurses

PRAYERS

Prayer to Saint Agatha
Dear Virgin and Martyr, whom the Church recalls in her liturgy, you heroically resisted the temptations of a degenerate ruler. Subjected to long and horrible tortures, you remained faithful to your heavenly Spouse. Saint Peter, we are told, gave you some solace and so you are invoked by nurses. Encourage them to see Christ in the sick and to render true service to them. Amen.

17
Saint Catherine of Siena

Patronage: against bodily ills, against fire, against illness, against miscarriages, against sexual temptation, against sickness, against temptations, Europe, fire prevention, firefighters, Italy, nurses, nursing services, people ridiculed for their piety, and sick people

PRAYERS

Prayer to Saint Catherine of Sienna
Humble virgin and Doctor of the Church, in thirty-three years you achieved great perfection and became the counselor of Popes. You know the temptations of mothers today as well as the dangers that await unborn infants. Intercede for me that I may avoid miscarriage and bring forth a healthy baby who will become a true child of God. Also pray for all mothers, that they may not resort to abortion but help bring a new life into the world. Amen.

Prayer to Saint Catherine of Siena
Dominican Tertiary and Doctor of the Church, you were full of wisdom, the special gift of God, and you knew how to guide even Pontiffs, as well as how to extinguish fiery passions and restore true peace among people. How inspiring your spiritual writings and how heroic your abstemious life! Fires are today unfortunately all too common - including those caused by criminals. Please protect and encourage firefighters in their heroic efforts to save lives. Amen.

Prayer of Saint Catherine of Siena to the Precious Blood of Jesus
Precious Blood,
Ocean of Divine Mercy:
Flow upon us!
Precious Blood,
Most pure Offering:
Procure us every Grace!
Precious Blood,
Hope and Refuge of sinners:
Atone for us!
Precious Blood,
Delight of holy souls:
Draw us! Amen.

Novena Prayer to Saint Catherine of Siena
O marvelous wonder of the Church, seraphic virgin, Saint Catharine, because of your extraordinary virtue and the immense good which you accomplished for the Church and society, you are acclaimed and blessed by all people. Oh, turn your benign countenance to me who, confident of your powerful patronage, calls upon you with all the ardor of affection and begs you to obtain, by your prayer, the favors I so ardently desire.

You, who were a victim of charity, who in order to benefits your neighbor obtained from God the most stupendous miracles and became the joy and the hope of all, you cannot help but hear the prayers of those who fly into your heart - that heart which you received from the Divine Redeemer in a celestial ecstasy.

Yes, O seraphic virgin, demonstrate once again proof of you power and of your flaming charity, so that your name will be ever more blessed and exalted; grant that we, having experienced your most efficacious intercession here on earth, may come one day to thank you in heaven and enjoy eternal happiness with you. Amen.

18
Saint Peregrine Laziosi

Patronage: against cancer, against breast cancer, against open sores, against skin diseases, AIDS patients, cancer patients, sick people

PRAYERS

Prayer to Saint Peregrine
Saint Peregrine, you have given us an example to follow; as a Christian you were steadfast in love; as a Servite you were faithful in service; as a penitent you humbly acknowledged your sin; afflicted you bore suffering with patience. Intercede for us, then, with our heavenly Father so that we steadfast, humble and patient may receive from Christ Jesus the grace we ask.

Prayer to Saint Peregrine
Oh great Saint Peregrine, you who have been called "The Mighty" and "The Wonder-Worker" because of the numerous miracles which you have obtained from God for those who have had recourse to you. For so many years you bore in your own flesh this cancerous disease that destroys the very fiber of our being, and who had recourse to the source of all grace when the power of man could do no more. You were favored with the vision of Jesus coming down from His Cross to heal your affliction. Ask of God and Our Lady, the cure of these sick persons whom we entrust to you.
Aided in this way by your powerful intercession, we shall sing to God, now and for all eternity, a song of gratitude for His great goodness and mercy. Amen.

Prayer to Saint Peregrine
Dear Apostle of Emilia and member of the Order of Mary, you spread the Good News by your word and by your life witnessed to its truth. In union with Jesus crucified, you endured excruciating sufferings so patiently as to be healed miraculously of cancer in the leg. If it is agreeable to God, obtain relief and cure for { *name of patient*} and keep us all from the dread cancer of sin. Amen.

Prayer to Saint Peregrine
O glorious wonder worker, Saint Peregrine, you who answered the divine call with a ready spirit, forsaking all the comforts of a life of ease and all the empty honors of the world, to dedicate yourself to God in the Order of His most Holy Mother; you who labored manfully for the salvation of souls, merting the title *Apostle of Emilia*; you who in union with Jesus crucified, endured the most painful sufferings with such patience so as to deserve to be miraculously healed from an incurable wound in your leg by Him with a touch of His divine hand: obtain for us, we pray, the grace to answer every call from God; enkindle in our hearts a consuming zeal for the salvation of souls; deliver us from the infirmities that so often afflict our bodies; and obtain for us the grace of perfect resignation to the sufferings which may be sent to us; so may we, imitating your virtues and tenderly loving our crucified Lord and his sorrowful Mother, be enabled to merit glory everlasting in paradise. We ask this in the name of Jesus the Lord. Amen.

Novena to Saint Peregrine
Oh great Saint Peregrine, you who have been called "The Mighty" and "The Wonder-Worker" because of the numerous miracles which you have obtained from God for those who have had recourse to you. For so many years you bore in your own flesh this cancerous disease that destroys the very fiber of

our being, and who had recourse to the source of all grace when the power of man could do no more. You were favored with the vision of Jesus coming down from His Cross to heal your affliction. Ask of God and Our Lady, the cure of these sick persons whom we entrust to you.
Aided in this way by your powerful intercession, we shall sing to God, now and for all eternity, a song of gratitude for His great goodness and mercy. Amen.

19
Saint Germaine Cousin

Patronage: abandoned people, abuse victims, against bodily ills, against illness, against impoverishment, against poverty, against sickness, child abuse victims, disabled people, girls from rural areas, handicapped people, loss of parents, peasant girls, physically challenged people, poor people, shepherdesses, sick people, unattractive people, victims of abuse, victims of child abuse and young country girls

PRAYERS

Prayer to Saint Germaine
O Saint Germaine, look down from Heaven and intercede for the many abused children in our world. Help them to sanctify these sufferings. Strengthen children who suffer the effects of living in broken families. Protect those children who have been abandoned by their parents and live in the streets. Beg God's mercy on the parents who abuse their children. Intercede for handicapped children and their parents.
Saint Germaine, you who suffered neglect and abuse so patiently, pray for us. Amen.

20
Saint John of God

Patronage: against alcoholism, against bodily ills, against sickness, alcoholics, bookbinders, booksellers, dying people, firefighters, heart patients, hospitals, hospital workers, nurses, publishers, printers and sick people

PRAYERS

Prayer to Saint John of God
Dear Convert, after a sinful life, through the power of God's holy Word you learned to love your fellow human beings. Self-sacrificing, you founded the Society of Hospital Brothers. No wonder the Church made you the patron of patients and nurses. That is why we confidently have recourse to you. Please give assistance to { *name of heart patient*} , and teach us to be kind like you. Amen.

Prayer re Saint John of God
O God, You filled Saint John with the spirit of compassion. Grant that by practicing works of charity we may deserve to be numbered among the elect in Your Kingdom. Amen.

PART THREE

21
Saint Stanislaus Kostka

Patronage: against broken bones, aspirants to the Oblates of Saint Joseph and last sacraments

PRAYERS

Prayer to Saint Stanislaus Kostka
Dear Saint Stanislaus, angel of purity and sepaph of charity, I rejoice with you at your most happy death, which arose from your desire to contemplate our Lady in heaven, and was at length caused by the excess of your love for her. I give thanks to Mary because she thus accomplished your desires; and I pray you, by the luster of your happy death, to be my advocate and patron in my death. Intercede with Mary for me to obtain for me a death, if not all happiness like yours, yet calm and peaceful, under the protection of Mary my mother, and of you, my special patron. Amen.

Prayer for the Graces of Saint Stanislaus
O God, Who among the many wonders of Your wisdom endow some, even in tender years, with the grace of ripest holiness: grant under us, we beseech You, after the pattern of Blessed Stanislaus, to be instant in good works, and thus to make speed to enter into everlasting rest. Amen

22
Saint Pio of Pietrelcina

Patronage: Confessors, Catholic adolescents *and* civil defense volunteers.

PRAYERS

Prayer for the Intercession of Saint Pio
Dear God, You generously blessed Your servant, St. Pio of Pietrelcina, with the gifts of the Spirit. You marked his body with the five wounds of Christ Crucified, as a powerful witness to the saving Passion and Death of Your Son. Endowed with the gift of discernment, St. Pio labored endlessly in the confessional for the salvation of souls. With reverence and intense devotion in the celebration of Mass, he invited countless men and women to a greater union with Jesus Christ in the Sacrament of the Holy Eucharist. Through the intercession of St. Pio of Pietrelcina, I confidently beseech You to grant me the grace of (here state your petition). Amen.
Glory be to the Father and to the Son and to the Holy Spirit, as it was in the beginning, is now and ever shall be, world without end. Amen (Say three times)

Saint Pio's Prayer for Trust and Confidence in God's Mercy
O Lord, we ask for a boundless confidence and trust in Your divine mercy, and the courage to accept the crosses and sufferings which bring immense goodness to our souls and that of Your Church. Help us to love You with a pure and contrite heart, and to humble ourselves beneath Your cross, as we climb the mountain of holiness, carrying our cross that leads to heavenly glory. May we receive You with great faith and love in Holy Communion, and allow You to act in us as You desire for your greater glory. O Jesus, most adorable Heart and eternal fountain of Divine Love, may our prayer find favor before the Divine Majesty of Your heavenly Father.

23
Saint Michael the Archangel

Patronage: against danger at sea, against temptations, ambulance drivers, artists, bakers, bankers, banking, barrel makers, battle, boatmen, coopers, dying people, emergency medical technicians, EMTs, fencing, Greek Air Force, greengrocers, grocers, haberdashers, hatmakers, hatters, holy death, knights, mariners, milleners, paramedics, paratroopers, police officers, radiologists, radiotherapists, sailors, security guards, sick people, soldiers, storms at sea, swordsmiths and watermen

PRAYERS

Prayer to Saint Michael
Saint Michael, Archangel, defend us in battle. Be our defense against the wickedness and snares of the devil.
May God rebuke him, we humbly pray. And you, Prince of the heavenly host, by the power of God, thrust into Hell Satan and the other evil spirits who prowl the world for the ruin of souls. Amen.

Prayer to Saint Michael
Dear Saint Michael, your name means, "Who is like God?" and it indicates that you remained faithful when others rebelled against God. Help police officers in our day who strive to stem the rebellion and evil that are rampant on all sides. Keep them faithful to their God as well as to their country and their fellow human beings. Amen.

Prayer for Help against Spiritual Enemies
Glorious Saint Michael, Prince of the heavenly hosts, who stands always ready to give assistance to the people of God; who fought with the dragon, the old serpent, and cast him out of heaven, and now valiantly defends the Church of God that the gates of hell may never prevail against her, I earnestly entreat you to assist me also, in the painful and dangerous conflict which I sustain against the same formidable foe. Be with me, O mighty Prince! that I may courageously fight and vanquish that proud spirit, whom you, by the Divine Power, gloriously overthrew, and whom our powerful King, Jesus Christ, has, in our nature, completely overcome; so having triumphed over the enemy of my salvation, I may with you and the holy angels, praise the clemency of God who, having refused mercy to the rebellious angels after their fall, has granted repentance and forgiveness to fallen man. Amen.

Novena Prayer to Saint Michael the Archangel

Glorious Saint Michael, guardian and defender of the Church of Jesus Christ, come to the assistance of His followers, against whom the powers of hell are unchained. Guard with special care our Holy Father, the Pope, and our bishops, priests, all our religious and lay people, and especially the children. Saint Michael, watch over us during life, defend us against the assaults of the demon, and assist us especially at the hour of death. Help us achieve the happiness of beholding God face to face for all eternity. Amen.

Saint Michael, intercede for me with God in all my necessities, especially { *mention special petition*}. Obtain for me a favorable outcome in the matter I recommend to you. Mighty prince of the heavenly host, and victor over rebellious spirits, remember me for I am weak and sinful and so prone to pride and ambition. Be for me, I pray, my powerful aid in temptation and difficulty, and above all do not forsake me in my last struggle with the powers of evil. Amen.

Prayer to Saint Michael the Archangel

In the name of the Father, and of the Son, and of the Holy Spirit. Amen. Most glorious Prince of the Heavenly armies, Saint Michael the Archangel, defend us in our battle against principalities and powers, against the rulers of this world of darkness, against the spirit of wickedness in the high places. Come to the assistance of men whom God has created to His likeness and whom He has redeemed at a great price from the tyranny of the devil. The Holy Church venerates thee as her guardian and protector; to thee the Lord has entrusted the souls of the redeemed to be led into Heaven. Pray therefore the God of Peace to crush Satan beneath our feet, that he may no longer retain men captive and do injury to the Church. Offer our prayers to the most High, that without delay they may draw His mercy down upon us. Take hold of the dragon, that old serpent, which is the devil and Satan, bind him, and cast him into the bottomless pit so that he should no more seduce the nations. Amen.

Novena to Saint Michael the Archangel

Saint Michael the Archangel, loyal champion of God and His People. I turn to you with confidence and seek your powerful intercession. For the love of God, Who made you so glorious in grace and power, and for the love of the Mother of Jesus, the Queen of the Angels, be pleased to hear our prayer. You know the value of our souls in the eyes of God. May no stain of evil ever disfigure it beauty. Help us to conquer the evil spirit who tempts us. We desire to imitate your loyalty to God and Holy Mother Church and your great love for God and people. And since you are God's messenger for the care of His people, we entrust to you these special intentions: (*mention your needs*).

Lord, hear and grant our special intentions for this Novena that we bring before You.

Police Officer's Prayer to Saint Michael
Saint Michael, heaven's glorious commissioner of police, who once so neatly and successfully cleared God's premises of all its undesirables, look with kindly and professional eyes on your earthly force. Give us cool heads, stout hearts, and uncanny flair for investigation and wise judgment. Make us the terror of burglars, the friend of children and law-abiding citizens, kind to strangers, polite to bores, strict with law-breakers and impervious to temptations. You know, Saint Michael, from your own experiences with the devil, that the police officer's lot on earth is not always a happy one; but your sense of duty that so pleased God, your hard knocks that so surprised the devil, and your angelic self-control give us inspiration. And when we lay down our night sticks, enroll us in your heavenly force, where we will be as proud to guard the throne of God as we have been to guard the city of all the people. Amen.

Litany of Saint Michael the Archangel
Lord, have mercy on us. *Lord, have mercy.*
Christ, have mercy on us. *Christ, have mercy.*
Lord, have mercy on us. *Christ, have mercy.*
Christ, hear us. *Christ, graciously hear us.*
God the Father of Heaven, *Have mercy on us.*
God the Son, Redeemer of the world, *Have mercy on us.*
God the Holy Spirit, *Have mercy on us.*
Holy Trinity, One God, *Have mercy on us.*

Holy Mary, Queen of the Angels, *pray for us.*
St. Michael the Archangel, *pray for us.*
Most glorious attendant of the Triune Divinity,
Pray for us is repeated after each invocation
Standing at the right of the Altar of Incense,
Ambassador of Paradise,
Glorious Prince of the heavenly armies,
Leader of the angelic hosts,
Warrior who thrust Satan into Hell,
Defender against the wickedness and snares of the devil,
Standard-bearer of God's armies,
Defender of divine glory,
First defender of the Kingship of Christ,
Strength of God,
Invincible prince and warrior,

Angel of peace,
Guardian of the Christian Faith,
Guardian of the Legion of Saint Michael,
Champion of God's people,
Champion of the Legion of Saint Michael,
Guardian angel of the Eucharist,
Defender of the Church,
Defender of the Legion of Saint Michael,
Protector of the Sovereign Pontiff,
Protector of the Legion of Saint Michael,
Angel of Catholic Action,
Powerful intercessor of Christians,
Bravest defender of those who hope in God,
Guardian of our souls and bodies,
Healer of the sick,
Help of those in their agony,
Consoler of the souls in Purgatory,
God's messenger for the souls of the just,
Terror of the evil spirits,
Victorious in battle against evil,
Guardian and Patron of the Universal Church, *pray for us.*

Lamb of God, Who takes away the sins of the world,
Spare us, O Lord.
Lamb of God, Who takes away the sins of the world,
Graciously hear us, O Lord.
Lamb of God, Who takes away the sins of the world,
Have mercy on us.
Pray for us, O glorious Saint Michael, *That we may be made worthy of the promises of Christ.*

Let Us Pray: Sanctify us, we beseech Thee, O Lord, with Thy holy blessing, and grant us, by the intercession of Saint Michael, that wisdom which teaches us to lay up treasures in Heaven by exchanging the goods of this world for those of eternity, Thou Who lives and reigns, world without end. Amen. Relying, O Lord, upon the intercession of Thy blessed Archangel Michael, we humbly beg of Thee, that the Holy Eucharist in whose presence we kneel, may make our soul holy and pleasing to Thee. We ask this through Christ Our Lord. Amen.

24
Saint Philomena

Patronage: against barrenness, against bodily ills, against infertility, against mental illness, against sickness, against sterility, babies, children, desperate causes, forgotten causes, impossible causes, infants, lost causes, Living Rosary, newborns, orphans, poor people, priests, prisoners, sick people, students, test takers, toddlers, young people and youth

PRAYERS

Prayer to Saint Philomena
O most pure Virgin, glorious Martyr, Saint Philomena, whom God in His eternal power has revealed to the world in these unhappy days in order to revive the faith, sustain the hope and enkindle the charity of Christian souls, behold me prostrate at thy feet. Deign, O Virgin, full of goodness and kindness, to receive my humble prayers and to obtain for me that purity for which thou didst sacrifice the most alluring pleasures of the world, that strength of soul which made thee resist the most terrible attacks and that ardent love for our Lord Jesus Christ, which the most frightful torments could not extinguish in thee. So, that wearing thy holy cord and imitating thee in this life, I may one day be crowned with thee in heaven. Amen.

Prayer to Saint Philomena
O great Saint Philomena, glorious Virgin and Martyr, wonder-worker of our age, I return most fervent thanks to God for the miraculous gifts bestowed on thee, and beseech thee to impart to me a share in the graces and blessings of which thou hast been the channel to so many souls. Through the heroic fortitude with which thou didst confront the fury of tyrants and brave the frowns of the mighty rather than swerve from thy allegiance to the King of Heaven, obtain for me purity of body and soul, purity of heart and desire, purity of thought and affection. Through thy patience under multiplied sufferings, obtain for me a submissive acceptance of all the afflictions it may please God to send me and as thou didst miraculously escape unhurt from the waters of the Tiber, into which thou wert cast by order of thy persecutor, so may I pass through the waters of tribulation without detriment to my soul. In addition to these favours, obtain for me, O faithful spouse of Jesus, the particular intention I earnestly recommend to thee at this moment. O pure Virgin and holy Martyr, deign to cast a look of pity from Heaven on thy devoted servant, comfort me in affliction, assist me in danger, and above all come to my aid in the hour of death. Watch over the interests of the Church of God, pray for its exaltation and prosperity, the extension of the faith, for the Sovereign Pontiff, for the clergy, for the perseverance of the just, the

conversion of sinners, and the relief of the souls in purgatory, especially those dear to me. O great Saint, whose triumph we celebrate on earth, intercede for me, that I may one day behold the crown of glory bestowed on thee in Heaven, and eternally bless Him who so liberally rewards for all eternity the sufferings endured for His love during this short life. Amen.

Novena Prayer to Saint Philomena
O faithful virgin and glorious martyr, Saint Philomena, who works so many miracles on behalf of the poor and sorrowing, have pity on me. Thou knowest the multitude and diversity of my needs. Behold me at thy feet, full of misery, but full of hope. I entreat thy charity, O great saint! Graciously hear me and obtain from God a favorable answer to the request which I now humbly lay before thee *(make your request here)*. I am thoroughly convinced that through thy merits, through the scorn, the sufferings, the death thou didst endure, united to the merits of the passion and death of Jesus thy spouse, I shall obtain what I ask of thee and in the joy of my heart I will bless God, who is admirable in his saints. Amen.

Litany to Saint Philomena
Lord, have mercy on us. *Lord, have mercy.*
Christ, have mercy on us. *Christ, have mercy.*
Lord, have mercy on us. *Lord, have mercy.*
God the Father of Heaven, *have mercy on us.*
God the Son, Redeemer of the world, *have mercy on us.*
God the Holy Ghost, *have mercy on us.*
Holy Trinity one God, *have mercy on us.*

Holy Mary, Queen of Virgins, *pray for us.*
Saint Philomena, *pray for us.*
Saint Philomena, filled with the most abundant graces from your very birth, *pray for us.*
Saint Philomena, faithful imitator of Mary, pray for us.
Saint Philomena, model of Virgins, *pray for us.*
Saint Philomena, temple of the most perfect humility, *pray for us.*
Saint Philomena, inflamed with zeal for the Glory of God, *pray for us.*
Saint Philomena, victim of the love of Jesus, *pray for us.*
Saint Philomena, example of strength and perseverance, *pray for us.*
Saint Philomena, invincible champion of chastity, *pray for us.*
Saint Philomena, mirror of the most heroic virtues, *pray for us.*
Saint Philomena, firm and intrepid in the face of torments, *pray for us.*
Saint Philomena, scourged like your Divine Spouse, *pray for us.*
Saint Philomena, pierced by a shower of arrows, *pray for us.*
Saint Philomena, consoled by the Mother of God when in chains, *pray for us.*

Saint Philomena, cured miraculously in prison, *pray for us*.
Saint Philomena, comforted by angels in your torments, *pray for us*.
Saint Philomena, who preferred torments and death to the splendors of a throne, *pray for us*.
Saint Philomena, who converted the witnesses of your martyrdom, *pray for us*.
Saint Philomena, who wore out the fury of your executioners, *pray for us*.
Saint Philomena, protectress of the innocent, *pray for us*.
Saint Philomena, patron of youth, *pray for us*.
Saint Philomena, refuge of the unfortunate, *pray for us*.
Saint Philomena, health of the sick and the weak, *pray for us*.
Saint Philomena, new light of the church militant, *pray for us*.
Saint Philomena, who confounds the impiety of the world, *pray for us*.
Saint Philomena, who stimulates the faith and courage of the faithful, *pray for us*.
Saint Philomena, whose name is glorified in Heaven and feared in Hell, *pray for us*.
Saint Philomena, made illustrious by the most striking miracles, *pray for us*.
Saint Philomena, all powerful with God, pray for us.
Saint Philomena, who reigns in glory, *pray for us*.

Lamb of God, Who takest away the sins of the world, *spare us, O Lord*.
Lamb of God, Who takest away the sins of the world, *graciously hear us, O Lord*.
Lamb of God, Who takest away the sins of the world, *have mercy on us*.

V. Pray for us, Great Saint Philomena,
R. That we may be made worthy of the promises of Christ

Let us pray: We implore Thee, O Lord, by the intercession of Saint Philomena, Virgin and Martyr, who was ever most pleasing to Thy eyes by reason of her eminent purity and the practice of all the virtues, pardon us our sins and grant us all the graces we need *(and name any special grace you may require)*. Amen.

25
Saint Teresa of Avila

Patronage: against bodily ills, against headaches, against sickness, against the death of parents, lace makers, lace workers, people in need of grace, people in religious orders, people ridiculed for their piety and sick people

PRAYERS

Prayer to Saint Teresa of Avila for a Sick Person
Dear wonderful Saint, model of fidelity to vows, you gladly carried a heavy cross following in the steps of Christ who chose to be crucified for us. You realized that God, like a merciful Father, chastises those whom he loves - which to worldlings seem silly indeed. Grant to { *name of sufferer*} relief from great pains, if this is in line with God's plans.

Prayer to Redeem Lost Time
O my God! Source of all mercy! I acknowledge Your sovereign power. While recalling the wasted years that are past, I believe that You, Lord, can in an instant turn this loss to gain. Miserable as I am, yet I firmly believe that You can do all things. Please restore to me the time lost, giving me Your grace, both now and in the future, that I may appear before You in "wedding garments." Amen.

26
Saint Roch

Patronage: against cholera, against diseased cattle, against epidemics, against knee problems, against plague, against skin diseases and against skin rashes

PRAYERS

Prayer to Saint Roch for a Sick Person
Dear mendicant Pilgrim, you once took care of sufferers from the plague and were always ready to help other by kind service and fervent prayers. You

yourself had no home and you died in a dungeon. No wonder countless invalids have confidently invoked your help. Please grant a cure to *{ name of the sufferer}*, and help us all become spiritually healthy.

27
Saint Benedict Joseph Labre

Patronage: against insanity, against mental illness, bachelors, beggars, homeless people, mentally ill people, people rejected by religious orders, pilgrims, tramps and unmarried men

PRAYERS

Prayer to Saint Benedict Joseph Labre
Saint Benedict Joseph Labre, you gave up honor, money and home for love of Jesus. Help us to set our hearts on Jesus and not on the things of this world. You lived in obscurity among the poor in the streets. Enable us to see Jesus in our poor brothers and sisters and not judge by appearances. Make us realize that in helping them we are helping Jesus. Show us how to befriend them and not pass them by. Saint Benedict Joseph Labre, you had a great love for prayer. Obtain for us the grace of persevering prayer, especially adoration of Jesus in the Most Blessed Sacrament. Saint Benedict Joseph Labre, poor in the eyes of men but rich in the eyes of God, pray for us. Amen.

28
Saint Blasé

Patronage: against coughs, against goitres, against throat diseases, against whooping cough, against wild beasts, animals, builders, carvers, construction workers, healthy throats, stonecutters, veterinarians, wool-combers and wool weavers

PRAYERS

Prayer to Saint Blasé
O glorious Saint Blasé, who by thy martyrdom didst leave to the Church a precious witness to the faith, obtain for us the grace to preserve within ourselves this divine gift, and to defend, without human respect, both by word and example, the truth of that same faith, which is so wickedly attacked and slandered in these our times. Thou who didst miraculously restore a little child when it was at the point of death by reason of an affliction of the throat, grant us thy mighty protection in like misfortunes; and, above all, obtain for us the grace of Christian mortification together with a faithful observance of the precepts of the Church, which may keep us from offending Almighty God. Amen.

Prayer to Saint Blasé for Healing
Dear bishop and lover of souls, you willingly bore heavy crosses in faithful imitation of Jesus. Similarly, with Christlike compassion you cured many sufferers. Than after undergoing horrible torture, you died as a martyr for Christ. Obtain a cure for these { *describe the afflictions*} ills if this is agreeable to God. Amen.

Novena in Honor of Saint Blasé
Preparatory Prayer
Almighty and eternal God! With lively faith and reverently worshiping Thy divine Majesty, I prostrate myself before Thee and invoke with filial trust Thy supreme bounty and mercy. Illumine the darkness of my intellect with a ray of Thy heavenly light and inflame my heart with the fire of Thy divine love, that I may contemplate the great virtues and merits of the saint in whose honor I make this novena, and following his example imitate, like him, the life of Thy divine Son. Moreover, I beseech Thee to grant graciously, through the merits and intercession of this powerful Helper, the petition which through him I humbly place before Thee, devoutly saving, "Thy will be done on earth as it is in heaven." Vouchsafe graciously to hear it, if it redounds to Thy greater glory and to the salvation of my soul. Amen.

Prayer in Honor of Saint Blasé

O GOD, deliver us through the intercession of Thy holy bishop and martyr Blasé, from all evil of soul and body, especially from all ills of the throat; and grant us the grace to make a good confession in the confident hope of obtaining Thy pardon, and ever to praise with worthy lips Thy most holy name. We ask this through Christ our Lord.
Amen.

Invocation of Saint Blasé

Saint Blasé, gracious benefactor of mankind and faithful servant of God, who for the love of our Saviour didst suffer so many tortures with patience and resignation; I invoke thy powerful intercession. Preserve me from all evils of soul and body. Because of thy great merits God endowed thee with the special grace to help those that suffer from ills of the throat; relieve and preserve me from them, so that I may always be able to fulfil my duties, and with the aid of God's grace perform good works. I invoke thy help as special physician of souls, that I may confess my sins sincerely in the holy sacrament of Penance and obtain their forgiveness. I recommend to thy merciful intercession also those who unfortunately concealed a sin in confession. Obtain for them the grace to accuse themselves sincerely and contritely of the sin they concealed, of the sacrilegious confessions and communions they made, and of all the sins they committed since then, so that they may receive pardon, the grace of God, and the remission of the eternal punishment.
Amen.

My Lord and my God! I offer up to Thee my petition in union with the bitter passion and death of Jesus Christ, Thy Son, together with the merits of His immaculate and blessed Mother, Mary ever virgin, and of all the saints, particularly with those of the holy Helper in whose honor I make this novena. Look down upon me, merciful Lord! Grant me Thy grace and Thy love, and graciously hear my prayer. Amen.

29
Saint Vincent de Paul

Patronage: against leprosy, Brothers of Charity, charitable societies, charitable workers, charities, horses, hospital workers, hospitals, lepers, lost articles, Madagascar, prisoners, spiritual help, Saint Vincent de Paul Societies, Sisters of Charity, Vincentian Service Corps and volunteers

PRAYERS

Prayer to Saint Vincent de Paul
Dear Saint, the mere mention of your name suggests a litany of your virtues: humility, zeal, mercy, self-sacrifice. It also recalls your many foundations: Works of Mercy, Congregations, and Societies. And the Church gratefully remembers your promotion of the priesthood. Inspire all Charitable Workers, especially those who minister to the poor – both the spiritually and the materially poor. Amen.

30
Saint Francis de Sales

Patronage: against deafness, authors, Catholic press, confessors, deaf people, educators, journalists, teachers and writers

PRAYERS

Prayer of Saint Francis de Sales
O love eternal, my soul needs and chooses you eternally!
Ah, come Holy Spirit, and inflame our hearts with your love!
To love – or to die!
To die – and to love!
To die to all other love in order to live in Jesus' love, so that we may not die eternally.

But that we may live in your eternal love, O Savior of our souls, we eternally sing,
Live, Jesus!
Jesus, I love!
Live, Jesus, whom I love!
Jesus, I love,
Jesus who lives and reigns forever and ever.
Amen.

Prayer of Saint Francis de Sales
Lord, I am yours, and I must belong to no one but you.
My soul is yours, and must live only by you.
My will is yours, and must love only for you.
I must love you as my first cause, since I am from you.
I must love you as my end and rest, since I am for you.
I must love you more than my own being, since my being subsists by you.
I must love you more than myself, since I am all yours and all in you.
Amen.

PART FOUR

31
Saint Andrew the Apostle

Patronage: against gout, against sore throats, anglers, fish dealers, fish mongers, fishermen, maidens, old maids, single lay women, singers, spinsters, unmarried women and women who wish to become mothers

PRAYERS

Prayer to Saint Andrew the Apostle
O Glorious Saint Andrew, you were the first to recognize and follow the Lamb of God. With your friend Saint John you remained with Jesus for that first day, for your entire life, and now throughout eternity.
As you led your brother Saint Peter to Christ and many others after him, draw us also to him. Teach us to lead others to Christ solely out of love for him and dedication in his service. Help us to learn the lesson of the Cross and to carry our daily crosses without complaint so that they may carry us to Jesus.

Prayer to Saint Andrew
Brother of Simon Peter, you heard John the Baptist say: "Behold the Lamb of God," and you chose to follow Jesus. Leaving your nets, you became a successful fisher of souls. Lover of the Crucified Christ, you too were crucified like him. Teach us to live and suffer for him and to win many souls for Christ.

32
Saint Ignatius of Antioch

Patronage: against throat diseases, Church in eastern Mediterranean and Church in North Africa

PRAYERS

Prayer for Martyrdom
I am the wheat of God, and am ground by the teeth of the wild beasts, that I may be found the pure bread of God.... I long after the Lord, the Son of the true God and Father, Jesus Christ. Him I seek, who died for us and rose again.... I am eager to die for the sake of Christ. My love has been crucified, and there is no fire in me that loves anything. But there is living water springing up in me, and it says to me inwardly: Come to the Father.
By Saint Ignatius of Antioch, Bishop and Martyr

33
Saint Anthony the Abbot

Patronage: against eczema, against epilepsy, against egotism, against erysipelas, against pestilence, against Saint Anthony's Fire, against skin diseases, against skin rashes, amputees, animals, basket makers, basket weavers, brush makers, butchers, cemetery workers, domestic animals, epileptics, gravediggers, graveyards, hermits, hogs, Hospitallers, monks, pigs, swine and swineherds

PRAYERS

Prayer to Saint Anthony the Abbott
Lord God, You gave Saint Anthony the Abbott the grace of serving in the desert in prayer with You. Aided by his intercession, may we practice self-denial and hence always love You above all things. Amen.

Prayer re Saint Anthony the Abbott
Father, you called Saint Anthony to renounce the world and serve you in the solitude of the desert. By his prayers and example, may we learn to deny

ourselves and love you above all things. We ask this through our Lord Jesus Christ, your Son, who lives and reigns with you and the Holy Spirit, one God, for ever and ever. Amen.

34
Saint Christopher

Patronage: against bad dreams, against epilepsy, against floods, against hailstorms, against lightning, against pestilence, against storms, against sudden death, against toothache, archers, automobile drivers, automobilists, bachelors, boatmen, bookbinders, bus drivers, cab drivers, epileptics, fruit dealers, fullers, gardeners, holy death, lorry drivers, mariners, market carriers, motorists, porters, sailors, taxi drivers, transportation, transportation workers, travellers, truck drivers, truckers and watermen

PRAYERS

Prayer to Saint Christopher
Dear Saint, you have inherited a beautiful name – Christbearer – as a result of a wonderful legend that while carrying people across a raging stream you also carried the Child Jesus. Teach us to be true Christbearers to those who do not know him. Protect all drivers who often transports those who bear Christ within them. Amen.

PRAYING WITH THE SAINTS

35
Saint Aloysius Gonzaga

Patronage: against sore eyes, AIDS care-givers, AIDS patients, Catholic youth, Jesuit students, teenage children, teenagers and young people

PRAYERS

Saint Aloysius' Prayer of Self-Commendation to Mary
O Holy Mary, my Lady, into your blessed trust and safe keeping and into the depths of yur mercy, I commend my soul and body this day, every day of my life, and at the hour of my death. To you I entrust all my hopes and consolations, all my trials and miseries, my life and the end of my life. By your most holy intercession and by your merits, may all my actions be directed and disposed according to your will and the Will of your divine Son. Amen.
By Saint Aloysius Gonzaga

Prayer to Saint Aloysius Gonzaga, Patron of Youth
Dear Christian youth, you were a faithful follower of Christ in the Society of Jesus. You steadily strove for perfection while generously serving the plague-stricken. Help our youth today who are faced with a plague of false cults and false gods. Show them how to harness their energies and to use them for their own and others' fulfillment - which will redound to the greater glory of God. Amen.

36
Saint Genesius of Rome

Patronage: actors, against epilepsy, attorneys, barristers, clowns, comedians, comics, converts, dancers, epileptics, lawyers, musicians, printers, stenographers and torture victims

PRAYERS

Prayer to Saint Genesius
Dear Genesius, according to a very ancient story, when you were still a pagan, you once ridiculed Christ while acting on the stage. But, like Saul on the road to Damascus, you were floored by Christ's powerful grace. You rose bearing witness to Jesus and died a great martyr's death. Intercede for your fellow actors before God that they may faithfully and honestly perform their roles and so help others to understand their role in life and thus enabling them to attain their end in heaven. Amen.

37
Saint John Chrysostom

Patronage: against epilepsy, Constantinople, epileptics, lecturers, orators, preachers, speakers

PRAYERS

Prayer to Saint John Chrysostom
Dear Saint John, your oratorical gifts inspired thousands and earned you the name "golden-mouthed." Continue to inspire Christians through your writings and grant us a rebirth of Christian preaching for the spiritual renewal of the Church. Obtain from God preachers like yourself who, animated by the Holy Spirit, deserve to be called other Christs and forcefully preach the Good News. Amen.

Prayer to Jesus before Holy Communion
O Lord, my God, I am not worthy that you should come into my soul, but I am glad that you have come to me because in your loving kindness you desire to dwell in me. You ask me to open the door of my soul, which you alone have created, so that you may enter into it with your loving kindness and dispel the darkness of my mind. I believe that you will do this for you did not

turn away Mary Magdalene when she approached you in tears. Neither did you withhold forgiveness from the tax collector who repented of his sins or from teh good thief who asked to be received into your kingdom. Indeed, you numbered as your friends all who came to you with repentant hearts. O God, you alone are blessed always, now, and forever.
By St. John Chrysostom

38
Saint Vitus

Patronage: actors, against animal attacks, against dog bites, against epilepsy, against lightning, against oversleeping, against rheumatic chorea, against snake bites, against storms, against wild beasts, comedians, Czech Republic, dancers, dogs and epileptics

PRAYERS

Prayer to Saint Vitus for Comedians
Dear Vitus, the one thing we are certain about is that you died a martyr's death. In early times, churches were dedicated to you in important places. In the Middle Ages, your intercession obtained cures from epilepsy so that this disease came to be called "Saint Vitus' Dance". Inspire comedians to make people dance with laughter and so bear goodwill toward one another. Amen.

39
Saint Thomas Aquinas

Patronage: academics, against storms, against lightning, apologists, book sellers, Catholic academies, Catholic schools, Catholic universities, chastity, colleges, learning, pencil makers, philosophers, publishers, scholars, schools, students, theologians, universities

PRAYERS

Prayer re Saint Thomas Aquinas
Father of wisdom, You inspired Saint Thomas Aquinas with an ardent desire for holiness and study of sacred doctrine. Help us, we pray, to understand what he taught, and to imitate what he lived. Amen.

Thanksgiving after Mass
Lord, Father all-powerful and ever-living God, I thank You, for even though I am a sinner, your unprofitable servant, not because of my worth but in the kindness of your mercy, You have fed me with the Precious Body and Blood of Your Son, our Lord Jesus Christ. I pray that this Holy Communion may not bring me condemnation and punishment but forgiveness and salvation. May it be a helmet of faith and a shield of good will. May it purify me from evil ways and put an end to my evil passions. May it bring me charity and patience, humility and obedience, and growth in the power to do good. May it be my strong defense against all my enemies, visible and invisible, and the perfect calming of all my evil impulses, bodily and spiritual. May it unite me more closely to you, the one true God, and lead me safely through death to everlasting happiness with You. And I pray that You will lead me, a sinner, to the banquet where you, with Your Son and holy Spirit, are true and perfect light, total fulfillment, everlasting joy, gladness without end, and perfect happiness to your saints. Grant this through Christ our Lord. Amen.
By Saint Thomas Aquinas

40
Saint Joseph

Patronage: against doubt, against hesitation, bursars, cabinetmakers, carpenters, Catholic Church, civil engineers, confectioners, craftsmen, dying people, emigrants, expectant mothers, families, fathers, happy death, holy death, house hunters, immigrants, interior souls, laborers, married people, Oblates of Saint Joseph, people in doubt, people who fight Communism, pioneers, pregnant women, protection of the Church, social justice, travellers, unborn children and workers

PRAYERS

Prayer to Saint Joseph
Blessed Joseph, husband of Mary, be with us this day. You protected and cherished the Virgin; loving the Child Jesus as your Son, you rescued Him from the danger of death. Defend the Church, the household of God, purchased by the blood of Christ. Guardian of the Holy Family, be with us in our trials. May your prayers obtain for us the strength to flee from error and wrestle with the powers of corruption so that in life we may grow in holiness and in death rejoice in the crown of victory.
Amen.

Prayer to Saint Joseph
Glorious Saint Joseph, foster-father and protector of Jesus Christ, to you I raise my heart and my hands to implore your powerful intercession. Please obtain for me from the kind Heart of Jesus the help and the graces necessary for my spiritual and temporal welfare. I ask particularly for the grace of a happy death and the special favor I now implore. *{ mention your petition}* Guardian of the Word Incarnate, I feel animated with confidence that your prayers in my behalf will be graciously heard before the throne of God. O glorious Saint Joseph, through the love you bear to Jesus Christ, and for the glory of His name, hear my prayers and obtain my petitions.

Prayer to Saint Joseph
O Saint Joseph, whose protection is so great, so strong, so prompt before the throne of God, I place in you all my interests and desires. O Saint Joseph, assist me by your powerful intercession and obtain for me from your Divine Son all spiritual blessings through Jesus Christ, Our Lord; so that having engaged here below your heavenly power I may offer my thanksgiving and homage to the most loving of Fathers.
O Saint Joseph, I never weary contemplating you and Jesus asleep in your arms; I dare not approach while He reposes near your heart. Press Him in my

name and kiss His fine head for me, and ask Him to return the Kiss when I draw my dying breath Saint Joseph, Patron of departing souls, pray for us. Amen.

Prayer to Saint Joseph before Mass
O Blessed Joseph, happy man, to whom it was given not only to see and to hear that God Whom many kings longed to see, and saw not, to hear, and heard not; but also to carry Him in your arms, to embrace Him, to clothe Him, and guard and defend Him.

V. Pray for us, O Blessed Joseph.
R. That we may be made worthy of the promises of Christ.

Let Us Pray: O God, Who has given us a royal priesthood, we beseech Thee, that as Blessed Joseph was found worthy to touch with his hands, and to bear in his arms, Thy only-begotten Son, born of the Virgin Mary, so may we be made fit, by cleanness of heart and blamelessness of life, to minister at Thy holy altar; may we, this day, with reverent devotion partake of the Sacred Body and Blood of Your Only begotten
Son, and may we in the world to come be accounted worthy of receiving an everlasting reward. We pray through the same Christ our Lord. Amen.

Prayer to Saint Joseph to Know One's Vocation
O Great Saint Joseph, you were completely obedient to the guidance of the Holy Spirit. Obtain for me the grace to know the state of life that God in his providence has chosen for me. Since my happiness on earth, and perhaps even my final happiness in heaven, depends on this choice, let me not be deceived in making it.
Obtain for me the light to know God's Will, to carry it out faithfully, and to choose the vocation which will lead me to a happy eternity.

Prayer to Saint Joseph for a Happy Death
O Blessed Joseph, you gave your last breath in the loving embrace of Jesus and Mary. When the seal of death shall close my life, come with Jesus and Mary to aid me. Obtain for me this solace for that hour - to die with their holy arms around me. Jesus, Mary and Joseph, I commend my soul, living and dying, into your sacred arms. Amen.

Prayer to Saint Joseph the Workman
We speak to you, O blessed Joseph, our protector on earth, as one who knows the value of work and the response of our calling. We address you through your holy spouse, the Immaculate Virgin Mother of God, and knowing the fatherly affection, with which you embraced Our Lord Jesus, ask

that you may assist us in our needs, and strengthen us in our labors. By our promise to do worthily our daily tasks, keep us from failure, from a greedy mind, and from a corrupt heart. Be our watchful guardian in our work, our defender and strength against injustice and errors. As we look to your example and seek your assistance, support us in our every effort, that we may come to everlasting rest with you in the blessedness of heaven. Amen.

Prayer to Saint Joseph
We come to you, O blessed Joseph, in our distress. Having sought the aid of your most blessed spouse, we now confidently implore your assistance also. We humbly beg that, mindful of the affection which bound you to the Immaculate Virgin Mother of God, and of the fatherly love with which you cherished the child Jesus, you will lovingly watch over the heritage which Jesus Christ purchased with His blood and by your powerful intercession help us in our urgent need. Prudent guardian of the Holy Family, protect chosen people of Jesus Christ; drive far from us, most loving father, all error and corrupting sin. From your place in heaven, most powerful protector, graciously come to our aid in this conflict with the powers of darkness, and as of old you delivered the Child Jesus from danger of death, so now defend the holy Church from the snares of the enemy and from all adversity. Extend to each one of us your continual protection, that, led on by your example, and borne up by your strength, we may be able to live and die in holiness and obtain everlasting happiness in heaven. Amen.

Prayer to Saint Joseph for Protection
Gracious Saint Joseph, protect me and my family from all evil as you did the Holy Family. Kindly keep us ever united in the love of Christ, ever fervent in imitation of the virtue of our Blessed Lady, your sinless spouse, and always faithful in devotion to you. Amen.

Novena to Saint Joseph
1st Day - Foster-Father of Jesus
Saint Joseph, you were privileged to share in the mystery of the Incarnation as the foster-father of Jesus. Mary alone was directly connected with the fulfillment of the mystery, in that she gave her consent to Christ's conception and allowed the Holy Spirit to form the sacred humanity of Jesus from her blood. You had a part in this mystery in an indirect manner, by fulfilling the condition necessary for the Incarnation - the protection of Mary's virginity before and during your married life with her. You made the virginal marriage possible, and this was a part of God's plan, forseen, willed, and decreed from all eternity. In a more direct manner you shared in the support, upbringing, and protection of the Divine Child as His foster-father. For this purpose the Heavenly Father gave you a genuine heart of a father - a heart full of love and

self-sacrifice. With the toil of your hands you were obliged to offer protection to the Divine Child, to procure for Him food, clothing, and a home. You were truly the saint of the holy childhood of Jesus - the living created providence which watched over the Christ-Child.

When Herod sought the Child to put Him to death, the Heavenly Father sent an angel but only as a messenger, giving orders for the flight; the rest He left entirely in your hands. Then it was that fatherly love was the only refuge which received and protected the Divine Child. Your fatherly love carried Him through the desert into Egypt till all enemies were removed. Then on your arms the Child returned to Nazareth to be nourished and provided for during many years by the labor of your hands. Whatever a human son owes to a human father for all the benefits of his up-bringing and support, Jesus owed to you, because you were to Him a foster-father, teacher, and protector. You served the Divine Child with a singular love. God gave you a heart filled with heavenly, supernatural love – a love far deeper and more powerful than any natural father's love could be. You served the Divine Child with great unselfishness, without any regard to self-interest, but not without sacrifices. You did not toil for yourself, but you seemed to be an instrument intended for the benefit of others, to be put aside as soon as it had done its word, for you disappeared from the scene once the childhood of Jesus had passed. You were the shadow of the Heavenly Father not only as the earthly representative of the authority of the Father, but also by means of your fatherhood - which only appeared to be natural - you were to hide for a while the divinity of Jesus. What a wonderfully sublime and divine vocation was yours - the loving Child which you carried in your arms, and loved and served so faithfully, had God in Heaven as Father and was Himself God!

Yours is a very special rank among the saints of the Kingdom of God, because you were so much a part of the very life of the Word of God made Man. In your house at Nazareth and under your care the redemption of mankind was prepared. What you accomplished, you did for us. You are not only a powerful and great saint in the Kingdom of God, but a benefactor of the whole of Christendom and mankind. Your rank in the Kingdom of God, surpassing far in dignity and honor of all the angels, deserves our very special veneration, love, and gratitude.

Saint Joseph, I thank God for your privilege of having been chosen by God to be the foster-father of His Divine Son. As a token of your own gratitude to God for this your greatest privilege, obtain for me the grace of a very devoted love for Jesus Christ, my God and my Savior. Help me to serve Him with some of the self-sacrificing love and devotedness with which you have done so. Grant that through your intercession with Jesus, your foster-Son, I may reach the degree of holiness God has destined for me, and save my soul.

Daily Novena Prayer

Saint Joseph, I, your unworthy child, greet you. You are the faithful protector and intercessor of all who love and venerate you. You know that I have special confidence in you and that, after Jesus and Mary, I place all my hope of salvation in you, for you are specially powerful with God and will never abandon your faithful servants. Therefore I humbly invoke you and commend myself, with all who are dear to me and all that belong to me, to your intercession. I beg of you, by your love for Jesus and Mary, not to abandon me during life and to assist me at the hour of my death. Glorious Saint Joseph, spouse of the Immaculate Virgin, obtain for me a pure, humble, charitable mind, and perfect resignation to the divine Will. Be my guide, my father, and my model through life that I may merit to die as you did in the arms of Jesus and Mary.

Loving Saint Joseph, faithful follower of Jesus Christ, I raise my heart to you to implore your powerful intercession in obtaining from the Divine Heart of Jesus all the graces necessary for my spiritual and temporal welfare, particularly the grace of a happy death, and the special grace I now implore: *(Mention your request).*

Guardian of the Word Incarnate, I feel confident that your prayers in my behalf will be graciously heard before the throne of God. Amen.

Memorare

Remember, most pure spouse of Mary, ever Virgin, my loving protector, Saint Joseph that no one ever had recourse to your protection or asked for your aid without obtaining relief. Confiding, therefore, in your goodness, I come before you and humbly implore you. Despise not my petitions, foster-father of the Redeemer, but graciously receive them. Amen.

2nd Day - Virginal Husband of Mary

Saint Joseph, I honor you as the true husband of Mary. Scripture says: **"Jacob begot Joseph, the husband of Mary, and of her was born Jesus who is called Christ"** (Matt. 1:16). Your marriage to Mary was a sacred contract by which you and Mary gave yourselves to each other. Mary really belonged to you with all she was and had. You had a right to her love and obedience; and no other person so won her esteem, obedience, and love. You were also the protector and witness of Mary's virginity. By your marriage you gave to each other your virginity, and also the mutual right over it - a right to safeguard the other's virtue. This mutual virginity also belonged to the divine plan of the Incarnation, for God sent His angel to assure you that motherhood and virginity in Mary could be united. This union of marriage not only brought you into daily familiar association with Mary, the loveliest of God's creatures, but also enabled you to share with her a mutual exchange of spiritual goods. And Mary found her edification in your calm, humble, and

deep virtue, purity, and sanctity. What a great honor comes to you from this close union with her whom the Son of God calls Mother and whom He declared the Queen of heaven and earth! Whatever Mary had belonged by right to you also, and this included her Son, even though He had been given to her by God in a wonderful way. Jesus belonged to you as His legal father. Your marriage was the way which God chose to have Jesus introduced into the world, a great divine mystery from which all benefits have come to us. God the Son confided the guardianship and the support of His Immaculate Mother to your care. Mary's life was that of the Mother of the Savior, who did not come upon earth to enjoy honors and pleasures, but to redeem the world by hard work, suffering, and the cross. You were the faithful companion, support, and comforter of the Mother of Sorrows. How loyal you were to her in poverty, journeying, work, and pain. Your love for Mary was based upon your esteem for her as Mother of God. After God and the Divine Child, you loved no one as much as her. Mary responded to this love. She submitted to your guidance with naturalness and easy grace and childlike confidence. The Holy Spirit Himself was the bond of the great love which united your hearts. Saint Joseph, I thank God for your privilege of being the virginal husband of Mary. As a token of your own gratitude to God, obtain for me the grace to love Jesus with all my heart, as you did, and you love Mary with some of the tenderness and loyalty with which you loved her.
(Daily Novena Prayer)

3rd Day - Man Chosen by the Blessed Trinity

Saint Joseph, you were the man chosen by God the Father. He selected you to be His representative on earth, hence He granted you all the graces and blessings you needed to be His worthy representative. You were the man chosen by God the Son. Desirous of a worthy foster-father, He added His own riches and gifts, and above all, His love. The true measure of your sanctity is to be judged by your imitation of Jesus. You were entirely consecrated to Jesus, working always near Him, offering Him your virtues, your work, your sufferings, your very life. Jesus lived in you perfectly so that you were transformed into Him. In this lies your special glory, and the keynote of your sanctity. Hence, after Mary, you are the holiest of the saints. You were chosen by the Holy Spirit. He is the mutual Love of the Father and the Son - the heart of the Holy Trinity. In His wisdom He drew forth all creatures from nothing, guides them to their end in showing them their destiny and giving them the means to reach it. Every vocation and every fulfillment of a vocation proceeds from the Holy Spirit. As a foster-father of Jesus and head of the Holy Family, you had an exalted and most responsible vocation - to open the way for the redemption of the world and to prepare for it by the education and guidance of the youth of the God-Man. In this work you cooperated as the instrument of the Holy Spirit. The Holy Spirit was the guide; you obeyed and carried out the works. How perfectly you obeyed the guidance of the God of Love! The words of the Old Testament which Pharaoh spoke concerning Joseph of Egypt can well be applied to you: **"Can we find such another man that is full of the spirit of God, or a wise man like to him?"** (Genesis 41.38)

No less is your share in the divine work of God than was that of Egypt. You now reign with your foster-Son and see reflected in the mirror of God's Wisdom the Divine Will and what is of benefit to our souls.

Saint Joseph, I thank God for having made you the man specially chosen by Him. As a token of your own gratitude to God, obtain for me the grace to imitate your virtues so that I too may be pleasing to the Heart of God. Help me to give myself entirely to His service and to the accomplishment of His Holy Will, that one day I may reach heaven and be eternally united to God as you are.

(Daily Novena Prayer)

4th Day - Faithful Servant

Saint Joseph, you lived for one purpose - to be the personal servant of Jesus Christ, the Word made flesh. Your noble birth and ancestry, the graces and gifts, so generously poured out on you by God - all this was yours to serve our Lord better. Every thought, word, and action of yours was a homage to the love and glory of the Incarnate Word. You fulfilled most faithfully the role of a good and faithful servant who cared for the House of God. How perfect was your obedience! Your position in the Holy Family obliged you to command, but besides being the foster-father of Jesus, you were also His disciple. For almost thirty years, you watched the God-Man display a simple and prompt obedience, and you grew to love and practice it very perfectly yourself. Without exception you submitted to God, to the civil rulers, and to the voice of your conscience.

When God sent an angel to tell you to care for Mary, you obeyed in spite of the mystery which surrounded her motherhood. When you were told to flee into Egypt under painful conditions, you obeyed without the slightest word of complaint. When God advised you in a dream to return to Nazareth, you obeyed. In every situation your obedience was as simple as your faith, as humble as your heart, as prompt as your love. It neglected nothing; it took in every command. You had the virtue of perfect devotedness, which marks a good servant. Every moment of your life was consecrated to the service of our Lord: sleep, rest, work, pain. Faithful to your duties, you sacrificed everything unselfishly, even cheerfully. You would have sacrificed even the happiness of being with Mary. The rest and quiet of Nazareth was sacrificed at the call of duty. Your entire life was one generous giving, even to the point of being ready to die in proof of your love for Jesus and Mary. With true unselfish devotedness you worked without praise or reward.

But God wanted you to be in a certain sense a cooperator in the Redemption of the world. He confided to you the care of nourishing and defending the Divine Child. He wanted you to be poor and to suffer because He destined you to be the foster-father of His Son, who came into the world to save men by His sufferings and death, and you were to share in His suffering. In all of these important tasks, the Heavenly Father always found you a faithful servant!

Saint Joseph, I thank God for your privilege of being God's faithful servant. As a token of your own gratitude to God, obtain for me the grace to be a faithful servant of God as you were. Help me to share, as you did, the perfect obedience of Jesus, who came not to do His Will, but the Will of His Father, to trust in the Providence of God, knowing that if I do His Will, He will provide for all my needs of soul and body: to be calm in my trials and to leave it to our Lord to free me from them when it pleases Him to do so. And help me to imitate your generosity, for there can be no greater reward here on earth than the joy and honor of being a faithful servant of God.
(Daily Novena Prayer)

5th Day - Patron of the Church

Saint Joseph, God has appointed you patron of the Catholic Church because you were the head of the Holy Family, the type and starting-point of the Church. You were the father, protector, guide and support of the Holy Family. For that reason you belong in a particular way to the Church, which was the purpose of the Holy Family's existence. I believe that the Church is the family of God on earth. Its government is represented in priestly authority which consists above all in its power over the true Body of Christ, really present in the Blessed Sacrament of the Altar, thus continuing Christ's life in the Church. From this power, too, comes authority over the Mystical Body of Christ, the members of the Church - the power to teach and govern souls, to reconcile them with God, to bless them, and to pray for them. You have a special relationship to the priesthood because you possessed a wonderful power over our Savior Himself. Your life and office were of a priestly functions are especially connected with the Blessed Sacrament. To some extent you were the means of bringing the Redeemer to us - as it is the priest's function to bring Him to us in the Mass - for you reared Jesus, supported, nourished, protected and sheltered Him. You were prefigured by the patriarch Joseph, who kept supplies of wheat for his people. But how much greater than he were you! Joseph of old gave the Egyptians mere bread for their bodies. You nourished and with tenderest care preserved for the Church Him who is the Bread of Heaven and who gives eternal life in Holy Communion. God has appointed you patron of the Church because the glorious title of patriarch also falls by special right to you.

The patriarchs were the heads of families of the Chosen People, and theirs was the honor to prepare for the Savior's incarnation. You belonged to this line of patriarchs, for you were one of the last descendants of the family of David and one of the nearest forebears of Christ according to the flesh.
As husband of Mary, the Mother of God, and as the fosterfather of the Savior, you were directly connected with Christ. Your vocation was especially concerned with the Person of Jesus; your entire activity centered about Him. You are, therefore, the closing of the Old Testament and the beginning of the New, which took its rise with the Holy Family of Nazareth. Because the New Testament surpasses the Old in every respect, you are the patriarch of patriarchs, the most venerable, exalted, and amiable of all the patriarchs. Through Mary, the Church received Christ, and therefore the Church is indebted to her. But the Church owes her debt of gratitude and veneration to you also, for you were the chosen one who enabled Christ to enter into the world according to the laws of order and fitness. It was by you that the patriarchs and the prophets and the faithful reaped the fruit of God's promise. Alone among them all, you saw with your own eyes and possessed the Redeemer promised to the rest of men.
Saint Joseph, I thank God for your privilege of being the Patron of the Church. As a token of your own gratitude to God, obtain for me the grace to live always as a worthy member of this Church, so that through it I may save my soul. Bless the priests, the religious, and the laity of the Catholic Church, that they may ever grow in God's love and faithfulness in His service. Protect the Church from the evils of our day and from the persecution of her enemies.
Through your powerful intercession may the church successfully accomplish its mission in this world - the glory of God and the salvation of souls!
(Daily Novena Prayer)

6th Day - Patron of Families
Saint Joseph, I venerate you as the gentle head of the Holy Family. The Holy Family was the scene of your life's work in its origin, in its guidance, in its protection, in your labor for Jesus and Mary, and even in your death in their arms. You lived, moved, and acted in the loving company of Jesus and Mary. The inspired writer describes your life at Nazareth in only a few words **"And (Jesus) went down with them and came to Nazareth, and was subject to them"** (Luke, 2:51). Yet these words tell of your high vocation here on earth, and the abundance of graces which filled your soul during those years spent in Nazareth. Your family life at Nazareth was all radiant with the light of divine charity. There was an intimate union of heart and mind among the members of your Holy Family. There could not have been a closer bond than that uniting you to Jesus, your foster-Son and to Mary, your most loving wife. Jesus chose to fulfill toward you, His foster-father, all the duties of a faithful

son, showing you every mark of honor and affection due to a parent. And Mary showed you all the signs of respect and love of a devoted wife. You responded to this love and veneration of both Jesus and Mary for you with feelings of deepest love and respect. You had for Jesus a true fatherly love, enkindled and kept aglow in your heart by the Holy Spirit. And you could not cease to admire the workings of grace in Mary's soul, and this admiration caused the holy love which you had consecrated to her on the day of your wedding you grow stronger every day. God has made you a heavenly patron of family life because you sanctified yourself as head of the Holy Family and thus by your beautiful example sanctified family life. How peacefully and happily the Holy Family rested under the care of your fatherly rule, even in the midst of trials. You were the protector, counselor, and consolation of the Holy Family in every need. And just as you were the model of piety, so you gave us by your zeal, your earnestness and devout trust in God's providence, and especially by your love, the example of labor according to the Will of God.

You cherished all the experiences common to family life and the sacred memories of the life, sufferings, and joys in the company of Jesus and Mary. Therefore the family is dear to you as the work of God, and it is of the highest importance in your eyes to promote the honor of God and the well-being of man. In your loving fatherliness and unfailing intercession you are the patron and intercessor of families, and you deserve a place in every home. Saint Joseph, I thank God for your privilege of living in the Holy Family and being its head. As a token of your own gratitude to God, obtain God's blessing upon my own family. Make our home the kingdom of Jesus and Mary – a kingdom of peace, of joy, and love.

I also pray for all Christian families. Your help is needed in our day when God's enemy has directed his attack against the family in order to desecrate and destroy it. In the face of these evils, as patron of families, be pleased to help; and as of old, you arose to save the Child and His Mother, so today arise to protect the sanctity of the home. Make our homes sanctuaries of prayer, of love, of patient sacrifice, and of work. May they be modeled after your own at Nazareth. Remain with us with Jesus and Mary, so that by your help we may obey the commandments of God and of the Church, receive the holy sacraments of God and of the
Church, live a life of prayer, foster religious instruction in our homes. Grant that we may be reunited in God's Kingdom and eternally live in the company of the Holy Family in heaven.
(Daily Novena Prayer)

7th Day - Patron of Workers

Saint Joseph, you devoted your time at Nazareth to the work of a carpenter. It was the Will of God that you and your foster-Son should spend your days together in manual labor. What a beautiful example you set for the working classes! It was especially for the poor, who compose the greater part of mankind, that Jesus came upon earth, for in the synagogue of Nazareth He read the words of Isaiah and referred them to Himself: **"The Spirit of the Lord is upon me; because He has anointed Me; to bring good news to the poor He has sent Me"** (Luke 4:18). It was God's Will that you should be occupied with work common to poor people, that in this way Jesus Himself might enoble it by inheriting it from you, His foster-father, and by freely embracing it. Thus our Lord teaches us that for the humbler class of workmen, He has in store His richest graces, provided they live in content in the place God's Providence has assigned them, and remain poor in spirit for He said, **"Blessed are the poor in spirit, for theirs is the kingdom of heaven"** (Matthew 5:3).

The kind of work to which you devoted your time in the workshop of Nazareth offered you many occasions of practicing humility. You were privileged to see each day the example of humility which Jesus practiced - a virtue most pleasing to Him. He chose for His earthly surrounding neither the courts of princes nor the halls of the learned, but a little workshop of Nazareth. Here you shared for many years the humble and hidden toiling of the God-Man. What a touching example for the worker of today!

While your hands were occupied with manual work, your mind was turned to God in prayer. From the Divine Master, who worked along with you, you learned to work in the presence of God in the spirit of prayer, for as He worked He adored His Father and recommended the welfare of the world to Him, Jesus also instructed you in the wonderful truths of grace and virtue, for you were in close contact with Him who said of Himself, **"I am the Way and the Truth and the Life."**

As you were working at your trade, you were reminded of the greatness and majesty of God, who, as a most wise Architect, formed this vast universe with wonderful skill and limitless power. The light of divine faith that filled your mind did not grow dim when you saw Jesus working as a carpenter. You firmly believed that the saintly Youth working beside you was truly God's own Son.

Saint Joseph, I thank God for your privilege of being able to work side by side with Jesus in the carpenter shop of Nazareth. As a token of your own gratitude to God, obtain for me the grace to respect the dignity of labor and ever to be content with the position in life, however lowly, in which it may please Divine Providence to place me. Teach me to work for God and with God in the spirit of humility and prayer, as you did, so that I may offer my toil in union with the sacrifice of Jesus in the Mass as a reparation for my sins, and gain rich merit for heaven.
(Daily Novena Prayer)

8th Day - Friend of Suffering

Saint Joseph, your share of suffering was very great because of your close union with the Divine Savior. All the mysteries of His life were more or less mysteries of suffering. Poverty pressed upon you, and the cross of labor followed you everywhere. Nor were you spared domestic crosses, owing to misunderstandings in regard to the holiest and most cherished of all beings, Jesus and Mary, who were all to you. Keen must have been the suffering caused by the uncertainty regarding Mary's virginity; by the bestowal of the name of Jesus, which pointed to future misfortune. Deeply painful must have been the prophecy of Simeon, the flight into Egypt, the disappearance of Jesus at the Paschal feast. To these sufferings were surely added interior sorrows at the sight of the sins of your own people.

You bore all this suffering in a truly Christ-like manner, and in this you are our example. No sound of complaint or impatience escaped you - you were, indeed, the silent saint!

You submitted to all in the spirit of faith, humility, confidence, and love; and cheerfully bore all in union with and for the Savior and His Mother, knowing well that true love is a crucified love. But God never forsook you in your trials. The trials, too, disappeared and were changed at last into consolation and joy.

It seems that God had purposely intended your life to be filled with suffering as well as consolation to keep before my eyes the truth that my life on earth is but a succession of joys and sorrows, and that I must gratefully accept whatever God sends me, and during the time of consolation prepare for suffering. Teach me to bear my cross in the spirit of faith, of confidence, and of gratitude toward God.

In a happy eternity, I shall thank God fervently for the sufferings which He deigned to send me during my pilgrimage on earth, and which after your example I endured with patience and heartfelt love for Jesus and Mary. You were truly the martyr of the hidden life. This was God's Will, for the holier a person is, the more he is tried for the love and glory of God. If suffering is the flowering of God's grace in a soul and the triumph of the soul's love for God, being the greatest of saints after Mary, you suffered more than any of the martyrs.

Because you have experienced the sufferings of this valley of tears, you are most kind and sympathetic toward those in need. Down through the ages souls have turned to you in distress and have always found you a faithful friend in suffering. You have graciously heard their prayers in their needs even though it demanded a miracle. Having been so intimately united with Jesus and Mary in life, your intercession with them is most powerful.

Saint Joseph, I thank God for your privilege of being able to suffer for Jesus and Mary. As a token of your own gratitude to God, obtain for me the grace to bear my suffering patiently for love of Jesus and Mary. Grant that I may

unite the sufferings, works and disappointments of life with the sacrifice of Jesus in the Mass, and share like you in Mary's spirit of sacrifice.
(Daily Novena Prayer)

9th Day - Patron of a Happy Death
Saint Joseph, how fitting it was that at the hour of your death Jesus should stand at your bedside with Mary, the sweetness and hope of all mankind. You gave your entire life to the service of Jesus and Mary; at death you enjoyed the consolation of dying in Their loving arms. You accepted death in the spirit of loving submission to the Will of God, and this acceptance crowned your hidden life of virtue. Yours was a merciful judgment, for your foster-Son, for whom you had cared so lovingly, was your Judge, and Mary was your advocate. The verdict of the Judge was a word of encouragement to wait for His coming to Limbo, where He would shower you with the choicest fruits of the Redemption, and an embrace of grateful affection before you breathed forth your soul into eternity.

You looked into eternity and to your everlasting reward with confidence. If our Savior blessed the shepherds, the Magi, Simeon, John the Baptist, and others, because they greeted His presence with devoted hearts for a brief passing hour, how much more did He bless you who have sanctified yourself for so many years in His company and that of His Mother? If Jesus regards every corporal and spiritual work of mercy, performed on behalf of our fellow men out of love for Him, as done to Himself, and promises heaven as a reward, what must have been the extent of His gratitude to you who in the truest sense of the word have received Him, given Him shelter, clothed, nourished, and consoled Him at the sacrifice of your strength and rest, and even your life, with a love which surpassed the love of all fathers. God really and personally made Himself your debtor. Our Divine Savior paid that debt of gratitude by granting you many graces in your lifetime, especially the grace of growing in love, which is the best and most perfect of all gifts. Thus at the end of your life your heart became filled with love, the fervor and longing of which your frail body could not resist. Your soul followed the triumphant impulse of your love and winged its flight from earth to bear the prophets and patriarchs in Limbo the glad tidings of the advent of the Redeemer.

Saint Joseph, I thank God for your privilege of being able to die in the arms of Jesus and Mary. As a token of your own gratitude to God, obtain for me the grace of a happy death. Help me to spend each day in preparation for death. May I, too, accept death in the spirit of resignation to God's Holy Will, and die, as you did, in the arms of Jesus, strengthened by Holy Viaticum, and in the arms of Mary, with her rosary in my hand and her name on my lips!
(Daily Novena Prayer)

Another Novena to Saint Joseph

Oh Saint Joseph whose protection is so great, so strong, so prompt before the Throne of God, I place in you all my interests and desires.

Oh Saint Joseph, assist me by your powerful intercession and obtain for me from your Divine Son all spiritual blessings through Jesus Christ, Our Lord; so that having engaged here below your Heavenly power I may offer my Thanksgiving and Homage to the Loving of Fathers.

Oh Saint Joseph, I never weary contemplating you and Jesus asleep in your arms. I dare not approach while He reposes near your heart. Press Him in my name and kiss His fine Head for me, and ask Him to return the kiss when I draw my dying breath.

Saint Joseph, Patron of departing souls, pray for us.

Amen

(Say for nine consecutive mornings for anything you may desire. It has seldom been known to fail.)

Litany of Saint Joseph

Lord, have mercy on us.
Lord, have mercy on us.
Lord, have mercy on us.
Christ, hear us. *Christ, graciously hear us.*
God, the Father of Heaven, *have mercy on us.*
God the Son, Redeemer of the world, *have mercy on us.*
God the Holy Ghost, *have mercy on us.*
Holy Trinity, one God, *have mercy on us.*

Holy Mary, *pray for us.*
Holy Joseph, *pray for us.*
Noble Son of the House of David, *pray for us.*
Light of the Patriarchs, *pray for us.*
Husband of the Mother of God, *pray for us.*
Chaste Guardian of the Virgin, *pray for us.*
Foster-father of the Son of God, *pray for us.*
Sedulous Defender of Christ, *pray for us.*
Head of the Holy Family, *pray for us.*
Joseph most just, *pray for us.*
Joseph most chaste, *pray for us.*
Joseph most prudent, *pray for us.*
Joseph most valiant, *pray for us.*
Joseph most obedient, *pray for us.*
Joseph most faithful, *pray for us.*
Mirror of patience, *pray for us.*
Lover of poverty, *pray for us.*

Model of all who labor, *pray for us.*
Glory of family life, *pray for us.*
Protector of Virgins, *pray for us.*
Pillar of families, *pray for us.*
Consolation of the afflicted, *pray for us.*
Hope of the sick, *pray for us.*
Patron of the dying, *pray for us.*
Terror of the demons, *pray for us.*
Protector of the holy Church, *pray for us.*
Lamb of God, you take away the sins of the world, *have mercy on us.*
Lamb of God, you take away the sins of the world, *have mercy on us.*
Lamb of God, you take away the sins of the world, *have mercy on us.*

He made him master of his house, *and ruler of all his possesions.*
Let Us Pray: O God, You were pleased to choose Saint Joseph as the husband of Mary and the guardian of your Son. Grant that, as we venerate him as our protector on earth, we may deserve to have him as our intercessor in heaven. We ask this through Christ our Lord. Amen.

PART FIVE

41
Saint Valentine of Rome

Patronage: affianced couples, against epilepsy, against fainting, against plague, apiarists, bee keepers, betrothed couples, engaged couples, greeting card manufacturers, greetings, happy marriages, love, lovers, travellers and young people

PRAYERS

Prayer for the Feast Day of St. Valentine
Grant, we beseech thee, O Almighty God that we who solemnize the festival of blessed Valentine, thy martyr, may, by his intercession, be delivered from all the evils that threaten us. I ask this through Christ Our Lord. Amen.

Prayer to St. Valentine
O glorious advocate and protector, St. Valentine, look with pity upon our wants, hear our requests, attend to our prayers, relieve by your intercession the miseries under which we labor, and obtain for us the divine blessing, that we may be found worthy to join you in praising the Almighty for all eternity: through the merits of Our Lord Jesus Christ. Amen.

St. Valentine's Prayer
Almighty God, grant we beseech You, that we, who honor the glorious martyrdom of St. Valentine, Your servant, may by his intercession be filled with the love of God and neighbor and be delivered from all the evils that threaten us. We ask this through Jesus Christ our Lord. Amen. *[Make the sign of the cross.]* St. Valentine, pray for us. *[State petition]* Amen.

Short Prayer to St. Valentine
Dear Saint and glorious Martyr; teach us to love unselfishly and to find great joy in giving. Enable all true lovers to bring out the best in each other in God and in God in each other.
Amen.

Prayer for St. Valentine's Day
Most Gracious Heavenly Father, You gave Saint Valentine the courage to witness to the gospel of Christ, even to the point of giving his life for it. Help us to endure all suffering for love of you, and to seek you with all our hearts; for you alone are the source of life and love. Grant that we may have the courage and love to be strong witnesses of your truth to our friends and

family and to the whole world. We ask this through our Lord Jesus Christ, your Son, who lives and reigns with you and the Holy Spirit, one God, for ever and ever.
Amen.

Another Prayer to St. Valentine
Dear Lord, who art high in the Heavens,
Giver of Love and Passion,
And He who strings the heart's cords,
Lead the Lovers this day, February ten plus four.
The day during the month of two,
When the date is the perfect number of God
Greater two souls and two hearts.
Some Loves are fleeting,
But that which is built on you will never fail.
So guide the Lovers to know what is to be.
Your truths the Lovers' mouths should speak,
For Your truth is that which is honest to the heart.
Only this, then, should pass over the red lips of the Lovers.
Your art, the Lovers simply a medium.
It is only with True Hearts that You can create a Masterpiece,
So let the Lovers remember that their Soul's Desire
Is the one for which You light their Fire.
And let it be You who creates the Art of the Lovers;
The art of two into one. Amen.

Prayer for the Intercession of Saint Valentine
Dear Jesus, I pray for the intercession of the beloved Saint Valentine, saint and glorious martyr, who is popular with lovers. I now pray humbly and urgently ask thy Father in thy name to hear my prayer and end my days of solitude and loneliness. Dear Father, send me someone who will return my affection as passionate as the summer sun. Dear Saint Valentine, I consecrate myself to thee, beseeching thee to number me among those whom you pray for with God in Heaven.
I will always remember in my heart that the more I honor you, the more you will bless me. Thank you for all the blessing to come my way. Amen.

42
Saint Martha of Bethany

Patronage: of housewives, of domestic workers, of servants and cooks

PRAYERS

Novena to Saint Martha of Bethany
[Light a candle]
O admirable Saint Martha, I have recourse to thee and I depend entirely on thy intercession in my trials. In thanksgiving, I promise to spread this devotion everywhere. I humbly beg thee to console me in all my difficulties. By the immense joy that filled thy soul when thou didst receive the Redeemer of the world at thy home in Bethany, be pleased to intercede for me and my family, in order that we may keep God in our hearts and therefore, deserve to obtain the remedy to our necessities, especially the present situation that overwhelms me. *[State intentions]* I implore thee, O Auxiliatrice in all needs; help us to overcome our difficulties, thou who so victoriously fought the dragon. Amen.
[Recite 3 times the following: 1 Our Father, 1 Hail Mary, 1 Glory Be, and the invocation "Saint Martha, pray for us." This Novena is prayed on 9 consecutive Tuesdays and involves lighting a candle. Pray also especially beginning 9 Tuesdays before July 29, the Feast of St. Martha.]

Prayer to Saint Martha
St. Martha, you are known as "The Lord's Worker and Servant." Help us to get out of our financial struggles. Enrich our lives, and help us decrease our debt. Help my children to be able to support themselves. Intercede with our Lord, Jesus, to be with my spouse, myself, and our children daily.
We will continue to praise, honor and adore you. Bless us, St. Martha; let us prosper in all areas of our lives. In the name of Jesus, I ask that we prosper financially. Amen.

Prayer to Saint Martha with Oil Lamp
St. Martha, I resort to thy protection and aid and as a proof of my affection and faith I offer this light in your lamp which I shall burn every Tuesday. Comfort me in all my difficulties, through the great favor thou didst enjoy when the Saviour was lodged in thy house. Intercede for my family that we may always hold God in our hearts, and that we may be provided for in all our necessities, I ask, St. Martha, to defeat all difficulties as thou didst defeat the dragon at thy feet. Amen.
[As a Novena, this may be said for nine Tuesdays, while burning a flame in an oil lamp, along with the Our Father, Hail Mary, and Glory be to the Father.]

Prayer to St Martha Patron Saint of Waitresses
O blessed St. Martha, I beseech thee to help me to serve others with just enough grace, humility and patience to garner a generous gratuity. Amen.

43
Saint Cecilia

Patronage: Academy of Music, Rome, composers, martyrs, music, musicians, musical instrument makers, poets and singers

PRAYERS

Prayer to Saint Cecilia
Dear Saint Cecilia, one thing we know for certain about you is that you became a heroic martyr in fidelity to your divine Bridegroom. We do not know that you were a musician but we are told that you heard Angels sing. Inspire musicians to gladden the hearts of people by filling the air with God's gift of music and reminding them of the divine Musician who created all beauty. Amen.

Prayer to Saint Cecilia
Pray for us Saint Cecilia. Inspire us with immortal fire; let music flow like powerful waters, that we sing and play beautifully as you did in your martyrdom. Bless us, Santa Cecilia, with the power of music, the universal language among men. Amen.

Prayer to St. Cecilia
O gentle Cecilia, sweet voice and melody of the Heart of Jesus. We come to you to beg your assistance. Pray for us Cecilia; teach us to sing to glories of God and also for the Glory of God. Give us the voice to sing the "Ave" as you did at the hour of your martyrdom. Pray for us o martyr with a singing heart. Amen.

Prayer to Saint Cecilia, Patron of Musicians
O sweet-voiced St. Cecilia, powerful patron and protectress, whose love for God was song in your heart, I ask your assistance. St. Cecilia, I ask your intercession because you generously offered the music in your heart and soul to Jesus. Our Lord will not refuse your prayers. Pray for me St .Cecilia. *(state petition.)* Amen.

Prayer Invoking the Intercession of St. Cecilia
O Eternal God, Who gave us, in the person of St. Cecilia, a powerful protectress, grant that after having faithfully passed our days, like herself, in innocence and holiness, we may one day attain the land of beatitude, where in concert with her, we may praise You and bless You forevermore in eternity. Amen.

Singers and Musicians Prayer to St. Cecilia
Pray for me St. Cecilia that I sing/play beautifully. Be with me in my hours of practice and when I perform. Especially help me with *(state petition)*. Amen.

44
Saint Jude Thaddeus

Patronage: difficult cases, hopeless cases, desperate situations, forgotten causes, hospital workers, hospitals, impossible causes and lost causes

PRAYERS

Prayer to Saint Jude
O, great Saint Jude
Whose traitor-sounding name
By man's perceptions crude
Confused is with the obloquy and blame
Of him who to our gain and his disaster
Betrayed so kind a Master;

We, seeing more clearly, concede thee what was thine;
The glory of a place beside that board
Whereon, awaiting their predestined hour
Of bowing to all-Good, all-Love, all-Power,
Lay bread and wine
Before that Host adored
Through whom our hope and our salvation came;
Thy kinsman, and our Lord.
O, thou, the sad day done,
Taking the homeward road
To thine obscure abode
In the long shadows of the setting sun,
To meet the frightened crowd
Sobbing aloud,
With thine Aunt Mary silent in their midst,
Leaning upon
The faithful arm of John;
Saint Jude, who didst
Join them in unbelief
And utter agony of grief,
And in a voice of pain and terror cried:
"Saw'st thou – and thou –
Saw'st thou indeed my Cousin crucified?"
O, by the memory of that hour of birth
Wherein Heaven's door opened to us of earth,
Befriend--befriend us now!

Prayer to Saint Jude
Most holy Apostle St. Jude, faithful servant and friend of Jesus, the name of the traitor who delivered the beloved Master into the hands of His enemies has caused you to be forgotten by many, but the Church honors and invokes you universally as the patron of hopeless cases, of things despaired of. Pray for me who am so miserable; make use, I implore you, of this particular privilege accorded to you, to bring visible and speedy help, where help is almost despaired of. Come to my assistance in this great need, that I may receive the consolations and succor of Heaven in all my necessities, tribulations and sufferings, particularly *(here make your request)*, and that I may bless God with you and all the elect forever.

I promise you, O blessed St. Jude, to be ever mindful of this great favor, and I will never cease to honor you as my special and powerful patron and to do all in my power to encourage devotion to you. Amen.

Prayer to Saint Jude Thaddeus
Glorious Saint Jude, with faith in your goodness I ask your help today. As one of Christ's chosen Apostles, you are a pillar and foundation of His Church on earth. You are among the elders who stand always before God's throne. Brother Jude, you are renowned for your kinship with Christ and your physical resemblance to our Savior. Help me remain close to Christ and resemble Him in my outlook and actions.
Holy Apostle, you are venerated for your work of preaching the gospel and your faithfulness to Christ by a martyr's death. Assist me to preach the good news of Christ by word and example, and remain steadfast in His service as you were. From your place of glory, do not forget the needs and difficulties of Christ's little ones like me, still struggling on the way home to God. Pray for me that I may receive the consolation and help of heaven in my necessities, tribulations and sufferings, particularly (name special problem) and that I may praise God with you and all the elect forever.
Intercede for us all, gracious brother Saint Jude, and pray for us to the Lord our God in our daily toil and our necessities.
Amen.

Prayer to Saint Jude the Apostle
O Glorious Saint Jude, you were honored to be a cousin as well as a follower of Jesus, and you wrote an Epistle in which you said: *"Grow strong in your holy faith through prayer in the Holy Spirit."* Obtain for us the grace of being people of faith and people of prayer. Let us be so attached to the three Divine Persons through faith and prayer on earth that we may be united with them in the glory of the beatific vision in heaven.

Prayer to Saint Jude
Dear Apostle and Martyr for Christ, you left us an Epistle in the New Testament. With good reason many invoke you when illness is at a desperate stage. We now recommend to your kindness { *name of patient*} who is in a critical condition. May the cure of this patient increase his/her faith and love for the Lord of Life, for the glory of our merciful God.
Amen.

Prayer to Saint Jude the Apostle
Glorious Apostle, Saint Jude Thaddeus, I salute you through the Sacred Heart of Jesus. Through His Heart I praise and thank God for all the graces he has bestowed upon you. I implore you, through His love to look upon me with compassion. Do not despise my poor prayer. Do not let my trust be confounded. God has granted to you the privilege of aiding mankind in the most desparate cases. Oh, come to my aid that I may praise the mercies of

God. All my life I will be your grateful client until I can thank you in heaven. Amen.
Saint Jude, pray for us, and for all who invoke your aid.

Prayer to Saint Jude Thaddeus
Most holy apostle, Saint Jude, faithful servant and friend of Jesus, the church honors you as member of the saint community with Saint Simon, apostle, on October 28 and invokes you universally, as the patron of hopeless cases, of things almost despaired of. Pray for us, we are so helpless and alone. Make use, we implore you, of that particular privilege given to you by God to bring visible and speedy help where help is almost despaired of. Come to our assistance in our necessities, creative work, tribulations and sufferings, particularly *(here make your request)* so that we may be better able to know, love and serve God with you and with all of God's people forever in accordance with God's Divine Will. We promise you, Oh blessed Saint Jude to be ever mindful of this great favor, to honor you as our special and powerful patron, and to gratefully encourage devotion to you, as favored servant to Jesus. May the most blessed heart of Jesus be adored as the Priest ordained Sacramental Presence in the Eucharist, and be received by the faithful Body of Christ throughout the world and through the Holy Spirit bring God's creation, including us undeserving servants, to perfection in God's name. Amen.

May the most sacred heart of Jesus be praised and glorified with the Father and Holy Spirit as One God in Holy Trinity, now and forever. Amen.

Blessed be the immaculate heart of Mary, Mother of God, assumed into Heaven, anticipating our bodily resurrection, and eternally glorified in Body and Soul with Her Son, Jesus
Christ. Amen.
Our Father, Hail Mary, and Glory be.

Novena to Saint Jude
To Saint Jude, Holy Saint Jude, Apostle and Martyr, great in virtue and rich in miracles, near kinsman of Jesus Christ, faithful intercessor of all who invoke your special patronage in time of need. To you I have recourse from the depths of my heart and humbly beg to whom God has given such great power to come to my assistance. Help me in my present and urgent petition, in return I promise to make your name known and cause you to be invoked. Saint Jude pray for us and all who invoke your aid. Amen.

45
Saint Gerard

Patronage: parenthood, for fruit of the womb, for safe delivery, against pregnancy complcations

PRAYERS

Prayer to St. Gerard for the Gift of a Child
O good St. Gerard, powerful intercessor before the throne of God, wonder-worker of our day, I call upon you and seek your help. While on earth, you always fulfilled God's designs; help me too, to always do God's holy will. Beseech the master of life, from whom all parenthood proceeds, to bless me with offspring, that I may raise up children to God in this life and as heirs to the kingdom His glory in the life to come. Amen.

Prayer to St. Gerard for Mother with Child
O almighty and everlasting God, through the Holy Spirit, you prepared the body and soul of the glorious Virgin Mary to be the lovely dwelling place of your divine Son. Through the same Holy Spirit, you sanctified St. John the Baptist, while still in his mother's womb. Hear the prayers of your humble servant who implores you, through the intercession of St. Gerard, to protect me amid the dangers of childbearing and to watch over the child with which you've blessed me. May this child be cleansed by the saving water of baptism and, after a Christian life on earth, may we, both mother and child, attain everlasting bliss in heaven. Amen.

46
Saint Rita of Cascia

Patronage: wives, widows, impossible cases, the needy

PRAYERS

Prayer to St. Rita for a Sufferer of Illness
Dear Rita, model wife and widow, you yourself suffered in a long illness, showing patience out of love for God. Teach us to pray as you did. Many invoked you for help, full of confidence in your intercession. Come now to my aid for the relief and cure of: *[Name of sufferer of illness]*. To God, all things are possible; may this healing give glory to the Lord. Amen.

Novena Prayer to St. Rita
[To be said for nine consecutive days, and then published if petition is granted]
O holy patroness of those in need, Saint Rita, whose pleadings before thy Divine Lord are almost irresistible, who for thy lavishness in granting favours hast been called the Advocate of the hopeless and even of the impossible; Saint Rita, so humble, so pure, so mortified, so patient and of such compassionate love for thy crucified Jesus that thou couldst obtain from Him whatsoever thou askest, on account of which all confidently have recourse to thee expecting, if not always relief, at least comfort; be propitious to our petition, showing thy power with God on behalf of thy suppliant; be lavish to us, as thou hast been in so many wonderful cases, for the greater glory of God, for the spreading of thy own devotion, and for the consolation of those who trust in thee.

We promise, if our petition is granted, to glorify thee by making known thy favour, to bless and sing thy praise forever. Relying then upon thy merits and power before the Sacred Heart of Jesus, we pray thee grant that… *[Make your request here]* as soon as God deems fit. Amen.

47
Saint Joan of Arc

Patronage: of martyrs, captives, France, militants, people ridiculed for their piety, prisoners, soldiers, Anglophobes, women appointed for voluntary emergency services and the Woman's Army Corps

PRAYERS

Prayer to Saint Joan of Arc
O Joan, holy liberator of France, the powerful holy force in the days of old, as you yourself said, "Peace would be found only at the point of a lance," who used the weapons of war when no other means were able to obtain a just Peace, take care and help today those who do not want to do violence and patiently try to employ all possible peaceful means of resolution, but now allow the violence of war.

Return, O great hearted Daughter of God, and wage war against the enemies of the people of France and the people of England, with whom you yourself wished an alliance for the good of humanity. Both nations are now raised for the defense of what you would have defended: *Justice between nations!* Both peoples wish to crush the rebirth of barbarism as they raise this cry which is yours: *Christianity must continue!*

Heroine of Orleans, transmit to our leaders, your talent to inspire your soldiers to accomplish great deeds of valor, in order that our soldiers' efforts will come to a rapid and successful end.

Triumphant One of Reims, prepare for us the just peace under the shield of a force that will be henceforth vigilant!

Martyr of Rouen, be near to all the soldiers who fall in battle, in order to support, console, and help them and those dear ones that they leave behind.

Saint of the Country, excite in all souls, in every home of the world, the zeal to contribute to the salvation of the world and the return of peace, works which you crave, the rediscovery of a more Christian life, through holy thoughts and actions, forgiveness and persistent prayer, that as you yourself once said, "God must be served first." Amen.

A Prayer to Saint Joan of Arc
Dear Saint Joan: I humbly ask you to help me to live as God wants me to. I would be happy if I had only a fraction of the love and kindness you had for your enemies as well as your friends. But most of all, I implore you to help me to obtain from God a spark of your great and endless love and faith so that I may truly love, serve and obey Him with my whole heart as you did to the very end of your holy life. May you always protect me and help me to stay pure in mind, body and spirit forever and ever. Amen.

Prayer to Saint Joan of Arc in Times of Trouble
Saint Joan of arc, give me strength!
In this, my time of need, I beg thee to come to my aid.
I humbly ask thee to help me bear my trials with honor,
As I remember you in your earthly agonies.
Blessed Joan, duty bound to god, give me courage!
You who left family and friends to enter into God's service,
Devout and valiant to uphold righteousness to the end,
While being insulted and harmed by your enemies.
Holy Joan, daughter of god, give me fortitude!
Help me to prevail in life and death over evil,
While bearing my injuries with the dignity you showed
When wounded in the breast, head, thigh, and heel.
Pious Joan, help me to be fearless!
Abandoned by the king you yourself had crowned,
Captured and sold to the highest bidder,
You put your trust in the King of Heaven to deliver you.
Venerable Joan, help me to be unwavering in my faith!
Beaten, bruised, questioned and accused,
You were denied that which you loved most:
Communion, confession, mass and public prayer.
Heroic Joan, help me to uphold justice!
Imprisoned, neglected, threatened and condemned,
Sentenced to die as a heretic the cruelest death,
To die by the fire and be raised up in heaven!
Glorious virgin, please intercede for me.
Hear this petition and my heartfelt plea.
Pray for me in this, my time of need,
For I believe God will deny you nothing. Amen.
(Here mention you specific request.)

Prayer to Saint Joan of Arc for Healing
Holy Saint Joan, compassionate to the sick and wounded, who, while on earth, nursed so many back to health, hear me.

You who wished to see no one injured or in discomfort, pray for me and guide me through this difficult time.

Daughter of God, wounded many times in battle, I petition you for healing *(here mention your request here)* so that I may be better able to serve God in whatever capacity HE wishes. Intercede for me.

It may not be in God's will for my body to be healed, for my sufferings may help another or my own soul. If my request is not granted, help me to remain strong, and instead be healed emotionally and spiritually. Amen.

A Prayer for Faith
In the face of your enemies, in the face of harassment, ridicule and doubt, you held firm to your faith. Even in abandonment, alone and without friends, you held firm in your faith. Even as you faced your own mortality, you held firm to your faith.

Dear Saint Joan, I pray that I maybe as bold in my beliefs as you were. I ask that you ride alongside me in all my battles. Help me be mindful that what is worthwhile can be obtained when I persist. Help me hold firm in my faith. Help me believe in my ability to act well and wisely. Amen.

A Prayer Composed By the Sisters of Saint Joan of Arc
O Saint Joan of Arc, courageous woman soldier, called by God to fight and save your country from the enemy; grant that I, like you, may hear God's call in my life and have the courage to follow it faithfully, as priest, religious, married or single. May your motto: 'My God must be first served,' be mine also; so that through me, He may build His kingdom here on earth. Intercede to the Master of the harvest, that He may send laborers into His harvest. Saint Joan of Arc, pray for us. Amen

Prayer to St. Joan of Arc
Oh, St. Joan of Arc, a little shepherdess, who later was to be called 'the Maid who would come to help the King of France' and boldly lead the men-at-arms in freeing Orleans from the English, I ask of you to intercede for me through Jesus Christ Our Lord, with the fervor and faithfulness you had when trying to accomplish the mission God, Our Heavenly Father had set before you, through the voices of St. Michael, St. Catherine and St. Margaret.

When on trial and asked, 'Do you believe you are in a state of grace?' You replied, 'If I am not, may God put me in it; and if I am, God keep me in it.' St. Joan of Arc, Patroness of France pray for me.

Prayer to St. Joan of Arc
St. Joan, always devout and pure, help me to be like you, to follow Our Lord's will, though sometimes difficult and unclear. I pray you to lend me your immense courage, a courage bestowed upon you by the Savior, in His

merciful love, that you might accomplish His will. St. Joan, shepherdess and leader of armies, lend me your great gift of courage that I might do Our Lord's Will as you have done it, no matter how difficult it may appear.

Prayer to St. Joan of Arc
Dear and Glorious St. Joan of Arc, my special patroness, friend and sister in Christ. I come before you this day to thank you for the graces you have obtained for me and my family and to ask your continued intercession with Our Lady to Jesus for us. Help me to fight the battles God sends me daily with the same courage and dedication you had. My battles may be smaller and different than the ones you were called to but I need the grace to surrender my will to God's daily. As you wore a physical armor, help me to put on the spiritual armor that St. Paul call us to wear in order to stay in the state of grace always. Be with me at my last hour so that my entry into eternity will be with faith in the divine Mercy of God no matter what form of death He wills for me. Help me to keep my eyes focused on Jesus and Him Crucified and Mary Immaculate. Grant me the signal grace I need at that hour and grant me the honor and privilege to stand next to you in the heavenly court with my family, St Joseph and all the saints and angels as we surround the thrones of Jesus and Mary through all eternity and worship the most holy and Triune God. St. Joan, virgin and martyr, pray for me. Amen

Prayer to St. Joan of Arc
Dear St. Joan: virgin, warrior and martyr; you who heard the voice of God so clearly and responded with your 'Yes'; you who diligently fought to prevent Satan from separating France, help me to hear the Voice of God as clearly as you did and help me to respond to Him with my Yes. I also ask you stop Satan from trying to separate me from God. I want so dearly to worship The Holy Trinity with Mary and you and all the Saints, for all eternity! I make this request in the Most Holy Name of Jesus Christ, our Lord and Savior! Amen!

A Soldiers Prayer to St. Joan
St. Joan of Arc, humble maiden of France, your heavenly Father miraculously endowed you with every military skill and knowledge, and raised you up as the Commander of the armies of France for the blessing of His Church, the protection of His people, and the glory of His Holy Name. By your merits and prayers may God also endow all military men and women with every military skill and knowledge necessary for his station of duty; may his mission always be righteous, and his actions always be courageous, compassionate, and just. And just as you showed your ardent love for Jesus in offering up your life for Him, so may they fulfill all that their duty requires. St. Joan of Arc pray for us that we may be made worthy of the promises of Christ. Amen.

St. Joan of Arc, Pray For Us
St. Joan of Arc, pray for us that we, like you, may receive the merciful gift of courage from Our Lord and Savior, Jesus Christ, to learn and do His will. St. Joan, pray for us that we, like you, may remain pure and steadfast in the face of all the temptations that we must endure in everyday life. St. Joan, pray for us that we, like you, may never lose sight of God's will, though we are persecuted and castigated by the world. And, finally, St. Joan, shepherdess, liberator and martyr, pray that we, also like you, may never lose our humanity and sense of humor in pursuing Our Lord's will.

The Litany of Saint Joan of Arc
Lord, have mercy on us!
Jesus Christ, have mercy on us!
Lord, have mercy on us!
Jesus Christ, hear us!
Jesus Christ, graciously hear us!
Our Heavenly Father, Who is God, *have mercy on us!*
Son, Savior of the world, Who is God, *have mercy on us!*
Holy Spirit, Who is God, *have mercy on us!*
Holy Trinity, Who is God, *have mercy on us!*
Holy Mary, virgin mother of God, *pray for us.*
Our Lady of the Assumption, principal patron of France, *pray for us.*
Saint Michael the Archangel, patron and special protector of France, *pray for us.*
Saint Catherine of Alexandria, virgin and martyr, *pray for us.*
Saint Margaret of Antioch, virgin and martyr, *pray for us.*
Saint Joan of Arc, chosen by God at Domremy, *pray for us.*
Saint Joan of Arc, informed [of her mission] by Saint Michael, the Archangel and his angels, *pray for us.*
Saint Joan of Arc, compliant to the call of God, *pray for us.*
Saint Joan of Arc, confidant [in] and submissive to her voices, *pray for us.*
Saint Joan of Arc, model of family life and labor, *pray for us.*
Saint Joan of Arc, faithfully devoted to Our Lady, *pray for us.*
Saint Joan of Arc, who delighted in the Holy Eucharist, *pray for us.*
Saint Joan of Arc, model of generosity in the service to God, *pray for us.*
Saint Joan of Arc, example of faithfulness to the Divine vocation, *pray for us.*
Saint Joan of Arc, model of union with God in action, *pray for us.*
Saint Joan of Arc, virgin and soldier, *pray for us.*
Saint Joan of Arc, model of courage and purity in the field [of battle], *pray for us.*
Saint Joan of Arc, compassionate towards all who suffer, *pray for us.*
Saint Joan of Arc, the pride of Orleans, *pray for us.*
Saint Joan of Arc, glory of Reims, *pray for us.*

Saint Joan of Arc, liberator of the Country, *pray for us*.
Saint Joan of Arc, abandoned and imprisoned at Compiegne, *pray for us*.
Saint Joan of Arc, pure and patient in your prison, *pray for us*.
Saint Joan of Arc, heroic and valiant before your judges, *pray for us*.
Saint Joan of Arc, alone with God at the hour of torment, *pray for us*.
Saint Joan of Arc, martyr of Rouen, *pray for us*.
Saint Joan of Arc and Saint Therese of Lisieux patronesses of France, *pray for us*.
All the Saints of France, intercede for us.
Lamb of God, Who take away the sins of the world, *have mercy on us, Lord*.
Lamb of God, Who take away the sins of the world, *graciously hear us, Lord*.
Lamb of God, Who take away the sins of the world, *have mercy on us, Lord*.
Saint Joan of Arc, pray for us, that we may become worthy of the promises of Our Savior Jesus Christ.

Let us pray.
Oh God, Who has raised up in an admirable manner, the virgin of Domremy, Saint Joan of Arc, for the defense of the faith and [our] country. By her intercession, we ask You that the Church [may] triumph against the assaults of her enemies and rejoice in lasting peace; through Jesus Christ Our Lord. Amen.

48
Saint Genevieve

Patronage: against plague, against disaster, against fever, Paris

PRAYERS

Prayer to Saint Genevieve
Saint Genevieve, you who by the days before, penance and prayer, ensured the protection of Paris, intercede near God for us, for our country, for the devoted Christian hearts; you who cured the sick and fed the hungry, obtain the light of God and make us stronger to reject temptation; you who had the

concern of the poor, protect the sick, the abandoned, and the unemployed; you who resisted the armies and encouraged the besieged, give us the direction for truth and justice; you who through the centuries never ceased taking care of your people, help us to keep the teachings of our Lord Jesus Christ. May your example be for us, an encouragement to always seek God and serve him through our brothers and sisters. Amen.

Litany to Saint Genevieve
Lord, have mercy on us.
Christ, have mercy on us.
Lord, have mercy on us.
Christ, hear us.
Christ, graciously hear us.
God the Father of heaven, *have mercy on us*.
God the Son, Redeemer of the world, *have mercy on us*.
God the Holy Spirit, *have mercy on us*.
Holy Trinity, one God, *have mercy on us*.
St. Genevieve, who since childhood was filled with God's grace, *pray for us*.
St. Genevieve, consecrated to Christ by St. Germane, *pray for us*.
St. Genevieve, obedient to the Holy Spirit, *pray for us*.
St. Genevieve, zealous defender of the faith, *pray for us*.
St. Genevieve, heroically devoted to the Church, *pray for us*.
St. Genevieve, whose life is an example how we should live for God, *pray for us*.
St. Genevieve, intercessor of the clergy, *pray for us*.
St. Genevieve, who suffered for your vocation, *pray for us*.
St. Genevieve, who knew about hostility and abandonment, *pray for us*.
St. Genevieve, who spent hours in prayer, *pray for us*.
St. Genevieve, whose fasts and prayers saved the city, *pray for us*.
St. Genevieve, who had a demanding friendship with the king, *pray for us*.
St. Genevieve, whose wisdom enlightened the pagans, *pray for us*.
St. Genevieve, whose prudence guided the leaders, *pray for us*.
St. Genevieve, with purity you overcame slander, *pray for us*.
St. Genevieve, whose strength stood up against the evil doers, *pray for us*.
St. Genevieve, who miraculously nourished the hungry, *pray for us*.
St. Genevieve, who reconciled sinners with God, *pray for us*.
St. Genevieve, who brought back to the Church the lost ones, *pray for us*.
St. Genevieve, who read the conscience through the gift of the Holy Spirit, *pray for us*.
St. Genevieve, who cured the sick, *pray for us*.
St. Genevieve, who controlled the floods, *pray for us*.
St. Genevieve, who restored peace between enemies, *pray for us*.
St. Genevieve, who softened the fate of the prisoners, *pray for us*.

St. Genevieve, who drove out demons, *pray for us.*
St. Genevieve, protector of your devoted people, *pray for us.*

Let us pray: Give us, Lord, the spirit of intelligence and love of which you filled your daughter, Genevieve, so that attentive to your service and seeking to do your will, we can please you by our faith and our deeds. We ask this through our Lord Jesus Christ, your Son, who lives and reigns with you and the Holy Spirit, one God, for ever and ever. Amen.

49
Saint Claire

Patronage: against eyes disease, for good weather, Assisi, embroiderers, gilders, gold workers, goldsmiths, laundry workers, needle workers, telegraphs, telephones, television, television writers

PRAYERS

Novena Prayers to Saint Claire for a Miraculous Intervention
God of mercy, you inspired Saint Claire with the love of poverty by the help of her prayers. May we follow Christ in poverty of spirit and come to the joyful vision of your glory in the kingdom of Heaven. I ask this through Jesus Christ your Son who lives and reigns with You and the Holy Spirit, One God forever and ever. Amen.
May the Sacred Heart of Jesus be praised, adored, glorified and loved today and everyday throughout the world forever and ever. Amen.
[Say this prayer whether you believe or not, and circulate or publish prayer on the 9th day. Ask for three favours: one normal request and two difficult cases. Say nine Hail Marys and the following prayers for nine consecutive nights in front of a lighted candle]

Another Novena to Saint Clare of Assisi
Invocation
O most Holy Trinity, Father, Son and Holy Spirit, we praise your Holy Name and the wonders of grace you worked in your servant, Saint Clare.

Through her powerful intercession grant us the favours we beg in this novena, above all the grace to live and die as she did in your most Holy Love. Amen.

First Day
O Seraphic Saint Clare, first disciple of the Poor Man of Assisi, who hast abandoned all riches and honours for a life of sacrifice and of highest poverty, obtain from God for us the grace we ask
(State your intention here...), that of always submitting to the Divine Will and of living confidently in the providence of our Heavenly Father. Amen.

Second Day
O Seraphic Saint Clare who, notwithstanding living separated from the world hast not forgotten the poor and the afflicted, but hast become a mother to them, sacrificing for them your riches and working for them innumerable miracles; obtain from God for us the grace we implore
(State your intention here...), Christian charity towards our brethren in all their spiritual and temporal needs. Amen.

Third Day
O Seraphic Saint Clare, light of your country, who hast delivered Italy from barbarous invaders; obtain from God for us the grace we implore
(State your intention here...), that of overcoming all attacks of the world against faith and morals thus preserving in our families true Christian peace with a holy fear of God and a devotion to the Blessed Sacrament. Amen.

Fourth Day
Blessed Saint Clare, whose very name means light, illumine the darkness of our minds and hearts so that we might see what God wishes us to do and perform it with a willing and joyful heart.
Before your birth, a Heavenly voice foretold that you would be a light illuminating the world.
Be a light to us in the sorrows and anxieties of this earthly life, and lead us into the eternal light of our home in Heaven. Amen.

Fifth Day
O Seraphic Saint Clare, whose virginal heart was great enough to love the whole world, take our petitions into your pure hands and present them to God. Pray for us that we may one day enter joyously before the throne of God. Let the light of your perfect purity consume the shadows of sin and corruption that darkens the world. Intercede by your innocence for our youth. Safeguard the peace of our homes and the unity of our family. Plead with your chaste love for all in peril. Amen.

Sixth Day
Generous Saint Clare, who left wealth and pleasure and all earthly goods to become the first spiritual daughter of Saint Francis and to serve God in the cloister, help us to commit our lives to God without limit or measure so that He may live in us and shine forth from us to all whose lives touch ours. You, who loved souls so much as to make your life a continual sacrifice for them, obtain for us the graces we now implore and win for us the strength to praise God in suffering as well as in joy. Amen.

Seventh Day
Faithful Saint Clare, loyal daughter of the Church, friend and confidante of popes, intercede for the holy Church and look graciously from Heaven on our Holy Father Pope. Enlighten us to remove from our souls all that hinders the progress of the Church on earth. Grant that we may share your great love for the church of God and spread His kingdom on earth by a holy life. You, who worked miracles in the presence of the pope on earth, obtain for us the graces we need, now that you stand in the presence of the most high God in Heaven. Amen.

Eighth Day
Valiant Saint Clare, who fearlessly stood alone against the barbarous Saracens, trusting in the Blessed Sacrament as your only protection, enkindle in us a tender love for Jesus Christ; help us to live Eucharistic lives. You who saved your city of Assisi from plunder and ruin, protect our city and archdiocese, plead for our beloved country and the suffering world. A voice from the Sacred Host rewarded your trust with a promise: "I will always take care of you." Glorious Saint Clare, from your high place in Heaven, take care of us now in our earthly needs and guide us by your light to Heaven. Amen.

Ninth Day
Gracious Saint Clare, who fulfilled your womanhood by a life of love in prayer and penance, help us to fulfill our destiny that we may one day greet you in Heaven. You who were consoled at your death by a vision of Christ band His Mother, obtain for us the grace that we may die under the special protection of God and enter into the life and bliss you now enjoy. Have pity on us who struggle, on us who mourn, and win for us the favours of God so that after this life we may come home to Him who lives and reigns forever and ever. Amen.

Closing Prayer
V. Pray for us, Saint Clare.
R. That we may be made worthy of the promises of Christ.

Let us pray: We pray You, Lord, grant us Your servants who celebrate the festival of Blessed Clare your virgin, by her intercession, to be partakers of the joys of heaven and coheirs with Your only-begotten Son, Who being God, lives and reigns forever and ever. Amen.

50
Saint Maria Goretti

Patronage: against poverty, against the death of parents, Albano, children, Children of Mary, girls, martyrs, poor people, rape victims, young people in general

PRAYERS

Prayer to Saint Maria Goretti
Charming Saint, and true child of Mary, Mother of Jesus, you were so young but already so strong in resisting a cruel tempter and preferring to die a martyr. How greatly we need today - when chastity is often discarded - more models and intercessors like you! Multiply faithful Children of Mary for her glory and that of her Son. Amen.

Prayer to Saint Maria Goretti
Saint Maria Goretti, strengthened by God's grace, you did not hesitate, even at the age of eleven, to sacrifice life itself to defend your virginal purity. Look graciously on the unhappy human race that has strayed far from the path of eternal salvation. Teach us all, and especially our youth, the courage and promptness that will help us avoid anything that could offend Jesus. Obtain for me a great horror of sin, comfort in the sorrows of life, and the grace which I earnestly beg of thee *(here insert intention)*, and that I may one day enjoy with thee the imperishable glory of Heaven. Amen.

PRAYING WITH THE SAINTS

ABOUT THE AUTHOR

Udeh Onyekachukwu Patrick is the Founder and President of the Catholic Poets Society, the Director of Arts Alliance Africa and a member of the African Research and Policy Analysis Group. He has a degree in Mass Communication, a Diploma in Management and a Proficiency Certificate in Conflict Analysis.
Patrick is a practicing Catholic with a strong devotion to saints. He lives with his family in Lagos, Nigeria.